Identify

And

Remove Curses

Gary V. Whetstone

Gary Whetstone Publishing
New Castle, Delaware

Gary Whetstone Publishing
P.O. Box 10050
Wilmington, DE 19850 U.S.A.
1 (302) 324-5400

Unless otherwise indicated, all Scripture quotations are from the King James Version of *The Holy Bible.*

Scripture quotations marked *(AMP)* are taken from *The Amplified Bible. Old Testament* copyright © 1965, 1987 by The Zondervan Corporation. *The Amplified New Testament* copyright 1958, 1987 by The Lockman Foundation. Used by permission.

Scripture quotations marked *(NKJV)* are taken from *The New King James Version.* Copyright © 1979, 1980, 1982, Thomas Nelson Inc., Publishers.

Scripture quotations marked *(NIV)* are taken from the HOLY BIBLE, NEW INTERNATIONAL VERSION®. Copyright © 1973, 1978, 1984 by International Bible Society. Used by permission of Zondervan Publishing House. All rights reserved.

ISBN 0-9664462-1-6

Identify

And

Remove Curses

*As the bird by wandering,
as the swallow by flying,
so the curse causeless shall not come.*
Proverbs 26:2

Contents

Introduction

Do you sense that you are missing out on God's best blessings? Do you feel limited from accomplishing His agenda for your life? Is there some area in which the enemy may have an unexplained strangle hold—maybe in your finances, health, family relationships, work, church, or another area? Do you believe you are doing everything you know to do, and still a particular area of your life remains under siege?

In this book, I want to help you break the power of every negative influence that keeps you captive. Today, you can be set free from the restraints that hold back God's blessings and keep you from accomplishing the plans He has for you. This book will enable you to understand the causes of your and others' behavior patterns and show you how to break the curses that have plagued your life.

You see, negative words can have a secret hold on your life—a grip so powerful that, if unchecked, it can control whether you succeed or fail. In our society, insecure people frequently attempt to achieve significance by putting others down. Often, instead of words to edify, exhort, comfort, and strengthen us, we hear malicious, negative words. These come from employers, coworkers, neighbors—even from friends, teachers, close family members, and yourself! Whether you realize it or not, those negative words are curses, which release power to demonic spirits to control your life—until you break them by the power of God's Holy Spirit.

In *Identify And Remove Curses*, we will deal with words, motivations, intentions, generational and organizational curses; the effect that comes when curses get hold of you; and how to get and stay free. I firmly believe that the healing you receive as you read these pages will change your life. No longer must you remain restricted and limited from achieving everything God has designed for you. Freedom and success can be yours in Jesus' Name!

1
Understand Curses
And How They Come

Do you realize that unseen forces have the power to bind and restrict your success? Yet, most people understand very little about these forces, called *curses*. People do not recognize Satan's power and tactics. A common misconception is that curses only occur in cultures steeped with witches, voodoo, and medicine men. However, the truth is that Satan knows no cultural boundaries. His curses affect people all across the world—including the United States—and in all levels of spiritual development. *Even strong, mature Christians can suffer from curses without ever realizing it.*

How, then, can we recognize these curses? Where do they come from? How do we get them? More importantly, how do we get *rid* of them? In this and the next chapter, we will study these topics according to the Bible, the Word of God. It is critical that you understand these foundational truths so you can fulfill God's agenda for your life and walk in all the blessings He has promised to you.

People commonly convey curses to us today through spoken negative words, generations, organizations, humanism, and Satanic spirits. Let's begin our study on these topics now.

Negative Words

Did you grow up in a family with conflict between brothers, sisters, parents, or other relatives; where people argued and spoke negative words in your home? As a child, did it take you

3

awhile to recover from feelings of oppression when others hurled negative words against you or someone else?

Currently, in your home, do family members voice fear and confusion, or speak harsh, negative words to each other? Do you frequently hear outbursts of anger and hurt? At work, school, or even church, do people ridicule or speak evil of you? Maybe at times people prejudge or detest you with bitter words of hatred and resentment.

These negative words can affect your life for days, months, and years. For example, words spoken against you as a child can still have their influence over you 40 years later. Yet, you may not recognize their hold. If you believe what people have said, you can be like a spinning top all your life—going around and around without direction—not knowing what to do next.

Competitive comparisons were strong in my home when I was growing up. Until I was about 16 years old, I was the favored child over my brother. (I lost this status at that point in my life.) Perhaps you found yourself in that favored position. Or, maybe you were on the other side of the comparison: the black sheep of the family, the one who never quite made it.

Words are like strings attached to everything you do. *Even as you try to obey God and apply His Word in your life, words from your past will affect you unless you know how to break their hold.*

These negative words are actually curses—proclamations of harm or ill will. A curse is a detesting that takes place, an abhorrence that puts down another person and inflicts evil. Remember, a curse isn't only spoken by a witch with a crooked finger and a wart on her nose! We have seen that it can come from anyone—perhaps unknowingly from your neighbor, employer, spouse, child, or even yourself. No matter what you have experienced or how you have grown up, you need to identify words of curse, then break and remove their influence from your life forever.

Our basic Scripture for this study is Proverbs 26:2.

As the bird by wandering, as the swallow by flying,

so the curse causeless shall not come.

Proverbs 26:2

This Scripture begins with the phrase: "As the bird by wandering...." Where I live, on the east coast of the United States, flocks of migratory birds are constantly overhead in early spring and again in the fall. The huge volumes of birds fly in one direction, when suddenly they turn in another direction and then in another. These birds "wander" until they get into the right wind stream that will take them to their destination.

The verse continues, "...as the swallow by flying." A swallow is a tiny bird that arrives so quickly at its destination that often you don't even see it coming.

The Word of God uses these examples of birds to show how curses can influence your life. Many times negative words or curses come bringing harm. You expect your life to go in a certain direction, but suddenly it changes course. Sometimes harm comes before you even realize where it came from.

The verse ends, "...so the curse causeless shall not come." This means that if the curse is devoid of cost, reason, or advantage, it cannot come. You see, without a cause or an advantage, curses cannot come into your life. However, if you give them opportunity and you don't know how to remove them, Satan will have his way in your life through curses.

To illustrate this, let's look at the sport of tennis. In a tied game, a player must earn two more points to win. It is better to have the *advantage* or be in the *ad* position; this means that you already have one of the final two points required. This one-point advantage entitles you to win the game if you get the next point. Likewise, without that "one-point advantage," a curse cannot come into your life. Don't give curses any advantages to come into in your life. Instead, *you* take the advantage.

How do you get the advantage over curses and negative words that others speak? How can you stay on course, without deviation and without birds making nests in your hair to torment and afflict you? How do you stay free of curses? Keep reading to discover the biblical answers to these questions.

What Authority Do Words Have?

First, you must understand how words create curses. The book of Proverbs says:

> A man's belly shall be satisfied with the *fruit of his mouth;* and *with the increase of his lips* shall he be filled. *Death and life are in the power of the tongue: and they that love it shall eat the fruit thereof.*
>
> Proverbs 18:20-21

This means that the words spoken about you will either benefit or become a detriment to your life. Every word produces fruit. What is inside fruit? Within fruit are seeds of reproduction. The seeds produced from words can infiltrate your life for good or evil. Have you ever noticed that family members often share the same demeanor and attitudes? This is because the seeds of words spoken in their family took root, multiplied, and bore fruit for generations.

Seeds from your past can haunt you. Have you ever received a call from someone who reminded you about your past? Then, when you hung up the telephone, did those spoken words remain with you for days or maybe even years? Or, have you ever seen someone who caused you suddenly to remember something negative about your past? Then, did you find that you couldn't look at the person in the eyes? Does your past have a hold on you?

Some of our greatest limitations in life are unseen. Often curses—which the enemy has sent through others to rule us—dictate our actions, beliefs, and the attitudes we portray. These unseen controls must be broken.

Have you ever known a worker who lives according to his "just-get-by" mentality? He probably grew up in an environment where he heard, "Oh, you really don't need to become knowledgeable about that. Just whatever you can do to get by will be good enough." Now, when he thinks about further education and training to accomplish the desire of his heart, he says, "Oh well, getting by is good enough for me. Just give me my paycheck, and I'll be happy." To his detriment, the seeds of negative words that this worker ingested in his past are reproducing themselves in his life, today. He is restricting himself by his own beliefs. Words are extremely powerful. They condition you for success or failure.

Recognize The Power Of Generational And Organizational Curses

Today, curses from previous generations cause many challenges in family relationships.

Thou shalt not bow down thyself to them [idols], nor serve them: for I the Lord thy God am a jealous God, *visiting the iniquity of the fathers upon the children unto the third and fourth generation of them that hate me.*

Exodus 20:5

Many are not aware of how other people confer curses to them. Although they could be free within minutes, most people stay bound all their lives with negative behaviors, traits, and motivations; weakness in character; and challenges. It doesn't take long to be free from a generational curse, but you must understand its origin and how to remove its roots.

This section will shed biblical light on the reality of generational and organizational curses. As we approach this topic, you need to take a vital—but perhaps uncomfortable—step: let down your guard. When delving into our family histories, many of us set up strong defense mechanisms. We don't like anyone to see how it really is "behind the scenes." We don't want to live in glass houses. Well, we will find out about the glass house your parents and grandparents lived in, and we will throw some stones. However, in Jesus' Name, we will

7

break all the power of the enemy and believe God for a tremendous deliverance. So be open and let down your guard. Let's believe God for significant freedom as a result of the revelation you receive. Pray this prayer as we begin this section:

Father, I am dependent on the revelation knowledge in Your Word. I know Your Word is like a hammer that breaks into pieces every resistance that has power to thwart and limit my life.

Spirit of the Lord, I know that You alone are qualified to teach and demonstrate the power of God's Word. I am not here simply to occupy space and time. I am here to step into greater liberty and fulfillment than I ever knew was possible—to experience Your dominion in my generation. I am dependent on Your anointing to break the yoke and remove the forces of torment and affliction that have come to me through past generations.

I submit myself to You now. I resist the devil, and he must flee. Thank You for your revelation knowledge in my life, today. In Jesus' Name. Amen.

Generational Curses Are Real

Are generational curses real or merely something that you pick up in life? Some people say, "You have a temper just like your father." Or, "You have a drinking problem like your grandfather." Or, "She's crazy just like her mother." We become accustomed to and regard many traits and character flaws as normal. We say, "Well, that's just how he is." This may not be true. Maybe it is how he has *become.* Curses convey to others in different ways.

Certain families suffer from the tragedy of multiple divorces. People in other families don't marry until they are 40 or 50 years old, because they fear relationships. Sometimes an economic curse can pass down through generations, or deep insecurities confer from generation to generation. Often, we don't realize where they originate or why these curses exist.

What Curses Have Previous Generations Passed To You?

We know that each of us is responsible for what we do, but we may not be responsible for what causes us to do it. Our forefathers passed down to us the curse of the law. Now, you might quote Galatians, which says:

> Christ hath redeemed us from the curse of the law, being made a curse for us: for it is written, Cursed is every one that hangeth on a tree:
> That the blessing of Abraham might come on the Gentiles through Jesus Christ....
>
> Galatians 3:13-14

Yes, Jesus became a curse to remove the curse of the law. *However, if you want to receive anything promised to you in the Bible, you must appropriate it by your actions of faith.* You do not engage the truth of God's Word in your life until you act upon it in faith. For example, the Bible says, that by the stripes of Jesus you "were healed" (1 Peter 2:24). Now, most people never receive their healings, because they fail to take that truth and appropriate faith to it. The Word of God says:

> Surely He has borne our griefs—sickness, weakness and distress—and carried our sorrows and pain [of punishment]. Yet we ignorantly considered Him stricken, smitten and afflicted by God [as if with leprosy].
>
> Isaiah 53:4 (AMP)

We see that Jesus carried away all pain and sickness; yet many of us never experience it, because we fail to act on it in faith. It's the same way with generational curses. You might say, "Jesus bore all the curse of the law. So it cannot be in my life." Well, the curse will be in your life until—like any other promise of God's Word—you put your faith into action.

Did you grow up in a godly family, dedicated to serving the

9

Lord, praying in the Spirit, and seeking God fervently? If you did not, then yours was a cursed family; and you can pass that curse to future generations. Moreover, you can be unaware of a curse in your life from 1,000 years ago. Maybe your forefathers passed down a curse to you because they hated the living God and died without serving Him. This is a sobering thought.

Let's look at what Moses wrote in Deuteronomy about curses to see if it applies to your family background.

But it shall come to pass, if thou wilt not hearken unto the voice of the Lord thy God, to observe to do all his commandments and his statutes which I command thee this day; that all these curses [proclamations of harm; declarations of ill will] shall come upon thee, and overtake thee.

Deuteronomy 28:15

Then, Moses listed the kinds of curses that result from disobedience and not seeking the Lord. Let's look at several:

Cursed shall be thy basket and thy store.

Deuteronomy 28:17

Is there financial or business failure in your ancestry?

And thy heaven that is over thy head shall be brass, and the earth that is under thee shall be iron.

Deuteronomy 28:23

Did your parents or grandparents live in mediocrity without significant success? Can you look back and see that heaven didn't give them breakthroughs? Did the earth fail to give them their rightful due? That is a curse.

The Lord shall cause thee to be smitten before thine enemies: thou shalt go out one way against them, and

10

flee seven ways before them: and shalt be removed into all the kingdoms of the earth.

Deuteronomy 28:25

This means that the devil has overthrown these people in "the battles of life," and they have not accomplished great feats. Have your parents achieved great dreams?

The Lord shall smite thee with madness, and blindness, and astonishment of heart.

Deuteronomy 28:28

Is there the curse of mental illness in your genealogy?

Thou shalt betroth a wife, and another man shall lie with her: thou shalt build an house, and thou shalt not dwell therein: thou shalt plant a vineyard, and shalt not gather the grapes thereof.

Deuteronomy 28:30

Is there divorce anywhere in your background? Remember, curses can go back to more than four generations.

Thou shalt carry much seed out into the field, and shalt gather but little in; for the locust shall consume it.
Thou shalt have olive trees throughout all thy coasts, but thou shalt not anoint thyself with the oil; for thine olive shall cast his fruit.

Deuteronomy 28:38, 40

Curses create great revenue loss. Did your parents or grandparents labor and not have excellent economic return from it?

Thou shalt beget sons and daughters, but thou shalt not enjoy them; for they shall go into captivity.

Deuteronomy 28:41

A family relationship that isn't joyful and harmonious is a curse that you can pass down to future generations.

> Moreover he will bring upon thee all the diseases of Egypt, which thou wast afraid of; and they shall cleave unto thee.
> Also every sickness, and every plague, which is not written in the book of this law, them will the Lord bring upon thee, until thou be destroyed.
> Deuteronomy 28:60-61

Muscular dystrophy, asthma, arthritis, heart disease, cancer and all kinds of genetic ailments can pass from one generation to the next. When you go to a doctor's office, he or she asks if your family has a history of heart problems, diabetes, and other diseases. Why? Medical research has proven that your parents can confer genetic inheritances to you. The Word of God confirms that generations do convey diseases genetically.

Unseen spiritual realities are at work in our lives. Medical science knows this is true. So does psychiatry. When you go through a psychological profile, the doctor asks about the psychological make-up of your parents. It is psychologically and sociologically known that you will adopt the behavior patterns and attitudes of your parents, and these will confer through you to your children. Curses do confer.

> Moreover all these curses shall come upon thee, and shall pursue thee, and overtake thee, till thou be destroyed; because thou hearkenedst not unto the voice of the Lord thy God, to keep his commandments and his statutes which he commanded thee:
> And they shall be upon thee for a sign and for a wonder, *and upon thy seed for ever.*
> Deuteronomy 28:45-46

Curses can stay in your family forever, until someone breaks them. Let it be you, today! Break all curses in Jesus' Name.

Sexual Sins Produce Generational Curses

Genesis 9 deals with Noah, his sons, and his grandson Canaan. Because of Ham's act of exposing his father's nakedness, Noah cursed Ham's son Canaan and his lineage. From Canaan came the Jebusites, Amorites, Girgasites, Hivites, Arkites, and the inhabitants of Sodom and Gomorrah. The curse came upon all the nations in the land of Canaan. Finally, God acted on the Canaanites' utter sinfulness and commanded Moses first, then Joshua, to kill them all—including wives, children, cattle, and everything that lived.

Perverted, homosexual, and promiscuous relationships of forefathers open the door to convey curses from one generation to the next. If not annihilated, that curse which came on you from previous generations, will ultimately come into you, your children, and their children. You have a responsibility to remove the Canaanite curse from your family completely.

Hosea addressed the spirit of whoredom. Notice how serious this is to God:

Whoredom and wine and new wine take away the heart.

My people ask counsel at their stocks, and their staff declareth unto them: for the spirit of whoredoms hath caused them to err, and they have gone a whoring from under their God.

They sacrifice upon the tops of the mountains, and burn incense upon the hills, under oaks and poplars and elms, because the shadow thereof is good: therefore your daughters shall commit whoredom, and your spouses shall commit adultery.

I will not punish your daughters when they commit whoredom, nor your spouses when they commit adultery: for themselves are separated with whores, and they sacrifice with harlots: therefore the people that doth not understand shall fall.

Hosea 4:11-14

13

Here we see a biblical principle. Once the spirit of the whore is in the parent, it confers to the other spouse and to their children. An adulterous relationship before marriage brings the spirit of adultery into that marriage. As a result, the couple produces adulterous children. Promiscuity in parents confers promiscuity to their children.

If you are thinking, *Not* my *children,* remember that those curses pass through all generations. They don't stop until the power of the curse is broken. They quit because you take your stand, decree, and break them by the power of the Holy Spirit.

You need to inform your children about how curses work and notify them of the curses that have been in your family. Make them abundantly aware so their spiritual guards are up, and conveyance of the curses cannot occur.

Curses Can Pass Through Organizations

Similarly, your association with a cursed *organization* or its *leader* can affect you negatively. A biblical example of this is Jeroboam, who became the head of the tribes of Israel. Read the story of this rebellious man in the books of 1 and 2 Kings and 1 and 2 Chronicles.

As a king and organizational leader, Jeroboam created an atmosphere of curse to which the whole nation fell prey. He built pagan altars; caused Israel to sacrifice to false gods; and appointed the lowest people as priests, rather than the Levites as God had ordained. Jeroboam's evil motivations led him to promote people for his own gain in the kingdom. He rebelled against those who were in right relationship with the Lord. Jeroboam sustained his position of influence by requiring the Israelites to sacrifice to pagan gods and not to the Lord God. This is an organizational curse.

The curse in Jeroboam's lineage carried on for four generations; and in the fourth generation, if a blood sacrifice did not stop the sin, it carried on four more generations. Rebellious pagan worship, false leadership, and false priesthood abounded. As you read 2 Kings 15:9, 18, 24, 28, you see that each man named fell to the curse:

> And he did that which was evil in the sight of the
> Lord, as his fathers had done: he departed not from the
> sins of Jeroboam the son of Nebat, who made Israel to
> sin.
>
> 2 Kings 15:9

When a rebellious-natured person starts a church, that spirit
of rebellion confers to the congregation. A sign of this is the
promotion of people to ministry offices for the pastor's own
gain rather than by God's ordination.

On the other hand, if a pastor starts a church in response to
the revelation of the Lord Jesus—out of a definitive call—as
God Himself purposed, then God's ordination releases the
power and life of the Holy Spirit into the congregation.

Before you join a church or an organization, always check its
origin to see if it is blessed or cursed. *This is a fundamental precept:
with everything you ever put your hand to, examine the origin, not
simply what is evident.* There is a big difference between the
origin and the apparent. Know the spirit that is behind the
operation.

Humanism—The Arm Of The Flesh

Many of us have grown up in a humanistic realm. I believe
that today our entire educational system is attempting to
persuade our youth to depart from God and to put their trust in
its secular humanism, which produces conditional ethics.
Humanists are teaching our young people to set up their own
ethical standards for what is true, valid, and right; instead of
relying on sound, biblical principles.

Society has trained us to develop trust in man's ability and
manmade opportunities; but this trust has imposed curses
upon us. Instead of relying on the truth of God's Word, we have
relied on man's wisdom. We have allowed our trust to become

distorted from a clear understanding of God's Word.

"Wilderness Teaching": A Curse
In the book of Jeremiah, we see the effect of a curse upon a person who trusted in man.

> Thus saith the Lord; *Cursed* be the man that trusteth in man, and maketh flesh his arm, and whose heart departeth from the Lord.
> For he shall be like the heath in the desert, and shall not see when good cometh; but shall inhabit the parched places in the *wilderness....*
>
> Jeremiah 17:5-6

Have you ever heard a "wilderness teaching?" It sounds like this: "Well, brother, these problems you are facing mean that you are in a wilderness time of your life. We all go through seasons in the wilderness. It's okay. Just trust that you'll come out some day."

Because we have learned to trust in ourselves, or "the arm of the flesh," we take on a cursed mentality and believe that being in the wilderness is normal. Do you realize that wilderness teaching is not in the New Testament? So, what kind of teaching did you hear? Cursed! You see, those of us who know the revelation of Jesus Christ should not go through any wildernesses. Jesus said:

> Howbeit when he, the Spirit of truth, is come, *he will guide you into all truth:* for he shall not speak of himself; but whatsoever he shall hear, that shall he speak: and he will shew you things to come.
>
> John 16:13

You have the Holy Spirit to guide you away from all wildernesses.

The sixth verse in Jeremiah 17 continues regarding "the man

16

that trusteth in man." The Word says that he:

...shall inhabit the parched places in the wilderness, in a salt land and not inhabited.

Jeremiah 17:6

Now, we know that one cannot plant or harvest in a salt land. It has no life, and no one can dwell there ever. Therefore, a curse, if it affects you, removes you from blessings. It removes from you the capacity of having a productive life. No longer do you have the motivation and desire to plant, sow, and reap.

On the other hand, the next two verses in Jeremiah 17 tell us how to live a blessed life:

Blessed is the man that trusteth in the Lord, and whose hope the Lord is.

For he shall be as a tree planted by the waters, and that spreadeth out her roots by the river, and shall not see when heat cometh, but her leaf shall be green; and shall not be careful in the year of drought, neither shall cease from yielding fruit.

Jeremiah 17:7-8

Which would you prefer: a barren life in a wilderness salt land or a fruitful, blessed life by the waters? It's your decision. *You* choose to trust in yourself and man's ways or to trust in the Lord. As for me and my house, we will trust in the Lord!

The Spirit Or Motive Behind Curses

Satanic Influence

The Church should be the most respectable entity that exists on the face of the earth; but the fact is, Satan has reproached God's covenant people since creation. He always has disdained and detested what God honors. The world today sneers at the sacredness of marriage, Christian values in child rearing, and

17

church attendance. Under Satan's influence, men and women speak words of ill will to reduce and minimize God's creation. Nevertheless, people curse themselves when they speak words— or even have thoughts, motivations or actions—against God and His values such as marriage, children, and the Church that Jesus died for. Anyone who speaks against the promises of God is a cursed person.

For example, let's study the Satanic influence that operated in the story of David and Goliath. We read in 1 Samuel:

> And David spake to the men that stood by him, saying, What shall be done to the man that killeth this Philistine, and taketh away the *reproach* from Israel? For who is this uncircumcised Philistine, that he should defy the armies of the living God?
>
> 1 Samuel 17:26

When someone reproaches you, he looks at you with disdain, dishonor, and disrespect. David understood that God intended for the nations of the earth to honor and respect Israel. David wasn't after Goliath. He merely wanted to remove the reproach from God's people, but Goliath happened to be in the way. Here is what David did next:

> And he took his staff in his hand, and chose him five smooth stones out of the brook, and put them in a shepherd's bag which he had, even in a scrip; and his sling was in his hand: and he drew near to the Philistine.
>
> And the Philistine came on and drew near unto David; and the man that bare the shield went before him.
>
> And when the Philistine looked about, and saw David, he *disdained* him: for he was but a youth, and ruddy, and of a fair countenance.
>
> And the Philistine said unto David, Am I a dog, that thou comest to me with staves? And the Philistine *cursed* David by his gods.

And the Philistine said to David, Come to me, and I will give thy flesh unto the fowls of the air, and to the beasts of the field.

Then said David to the Philistine, Thou comest to me with a sword, and with a spear, and with a shield: but I come to thee in the name of the Lord of hosts, the God of the armies of Israel, whom thou has defied.

This day will the Lord deliver thee into mine hand; and I will smite thee, and take thine head from thee; and I will give the carcases of the host of the Philistines this day unto the fowls of the air, and to the wild beasts of the earth; that all the earth may know that there is a God in Israel.

And all this assembly shall know that the Lord saveth not with sword and spear: for the battle is the Lord's, and he will give you into our hands.

1 Samuel 17:40-47

Goliath, under Satanic influence, cursed David by the gods, or demons, that he and his nation served. (The word *demon* means "a knowing being.") When a person speaks under the influence of a demonic spirit, he releases that demon's wicked and destructive force.

A combat of confidence took place. Goliath cursed David from the beings that he and his nation had confidence in. David was in covenant with the Lord of Hosts, the God of the armies of Israel; he knew in Whom he trusted and believed. David also knew that the Philistines abhorred his confidence in God. Unlike Goliath, David's was not a cursed mentality that trusted in the arm of the flesh. His was the blessed mentality that trusted the arm of the Lord!

We know the outcome of the story—David slung his rock, knocked Goliath down, and cut off Goliath's head with his own sword. This combat was not one of pride; it was a combat of confidence and recognition of that which God honors.

Another example of Satanic influence is Jezebel, who

worshiped the false god Baal. Married to Ahab, the king of Israel, she had great influence and authority even over the Prophet Elijah. Now, Elijah had killed the prophets of Baal during a showdown in which he proved theirs was a false god and the Lord God of Israel was the One True God.

And Ahab told Jezebel all that Elijah had done, and withal how he had slain all the prophets with the sword.

Then Jezebel sent a messenger unto Elijah, saying, So let the gods do to me, and more also, if I make not thy life as the life of one of them by to morrow about this time.

And when he saw that, he arose, and went for his life, and came to Beer-sheba, which belongeth to Judah, and left his servant there.

1 Kings 19:1-3

Here, we see that Elijah became unnerved and ran for his life. *A curse, by demonic operation, can, at times, overthrow the most intense strength of God's people.* We need to understand demonic curses and where they come from.

Although maybe not through a Goliath or the pagan wife of a king, today curses can come from Satanic influences such as witch doctors, black and white magic, mediums, palm readers, tarot cards, fortune tellers, zodiac charts, and those who commune with demonic spirits. When these people speak their forecasts to you or you read them, their curses are released against you.

Sometimes, entire nations are given over to the demonic operations of idolatry and witchcraft. For example, Brazil has plants that manufacture religious trinkets, over which people pronounce curses before exporting the items to the United States. They hide their evil purpose of spreading curses of disease, infirmity, and torment. Then, those who buy these trinkets unknowingly become infected with destructive curses.

I have been in crusades in many countries around the world. One time in Panama, I spent the night sleeping in a hammock in a witch doctor's hut, because it was the only place available. The witch doctor had a little fire going; he stayed up all night blowing curses and smoke over me and those who were with me so we would die by morning. He even called in rats to run all over the hut. When my companions woke me up, wondering what to do, I told them that I had prayed, and they should get some sleep. I said, "This guy is going to lose a whole night's sleep. You need to be alive and alert tomorrow, because we will win this place to the Lord." And win it we did!

Another night, I was on a crusade in Nigeria with my 9-year-old daughter and some others; we were having a significant impact in the city. A witch doctor, with a sheet over his head, came to my room and blew his incantations of smoke and curse, frightening my daughter. In Jesus' Name, we took authority over the demon spirit in him, and he fled.

When I was a child, my mother took me to mediums, who invoked curses upon me. Years later when I remembered this, I realized that I had to be set free of those curses; I did not want them to control my life. In the Name of Jesus, we broke those curses off my life.

Besides demonic activity, what are some other reasons that curses come into our lives? Next, we will examine several common motivations that cause people to curse us.

Man's Pride

The wicked, through the *pride* of his countenance, will not seek after God: God is not in all his thoughts.

His ways are always grievous; thy judgments are far above out of his sight: as for all his enemies, he puffeth at them.

He hath said in his heart, I shall not be moved: for I shall never be in adversity.

His mouth is full of *cursing* and deceit and fraud: under his tongue is mischief and vanity.

Psalm 10:4-7

21

Curses can come from an arena of pride. A prideful person believes he can operate in his own strength instead of in the Lord's strength. He puts his confidence in the flesh and thus curses himself. He is a fool who says, "I'm never going to go through difficulties in my life," as if his self-confidence can preserve him. People who are self-inflated with pride will curse. Why? It is because pride has to push someone down to lift itself up. Pride always must demean to elevate itself. If you get in the way of a prideful person, he is likely to put you down to lift himself up.

Bitterness, Envy, And Strife
We read in the book of James:

> Who is a wise man and endued with knowledge among you? let him shew out of a good conversation his works with meekness of wisdom.
> But if ye have *bitter envying and strife* in your hearts, glory not, and lie not against the truth.
> This wisdom descendeth not from above, but is earthly, sensual, devilish.
>
> James 3:13-15

The root word of *bitterness* means "wanting to cut or prick." When a seed or a root of bitterness is in a person, he loves to wound you to vindicate his own hurt. Someone who is bitter and hurt has a desire to cut. His words, then, are not gentle, caring, and loving. Instead, he speaks to slice, edge, and pierce others, because he loves to inflict harm to justify his own pain.

Envy is a contentious rivalry. When someone is envious of you, he feels that if you get ahead, he will be behind. He always feels he is in competition with you. He contends to be everything you are and to possess everything God has given to you. An envious person curses you in his words, thoughts, and actions.

Strife means "to be at odds with." When translated literally, it means, "a desire to put one's self forward." One of the interesting words from the Greek translation of *strife* is *electioneering,* the work of promoting a candidate or party in an election. We all know that to secure votes, an unethical candidate is likely to promise special concessions or positions to people. Some churches have begun in strife when the leadership promised positions to people, thus opening these church bodies to divisive spirits.

A person who electioneers to gain personal favor is in strife. He is also a curser—someone who speaks lies, deceit and hatred. Bitterness, envy, and strife fill his life. This type of person negatively influences others around him through his instability and confusion. He often misrepresents the Word of God for his own motivations. There is confusion in his every evil work and a state of disorder in his life.

> For where envying and strife is, there is confusion and every evil work.
>
> James 3:16

Wickedness, Deceit, Lies, and Hatred

> For the mouth of the *wicked* and the mouth of the *deceitful* are opened against me: they have spoken against me with a *lying* tongue.
> They compassed me about also with words of *hatred;* and fought against me without a cause.
> As he loved *cursing,* so let it come unto him: as he delighted not in blessing, so let it be far from him.
> As he clothed himself with cursing like as with his garment, so let it come into his bowels like water, and like oil into his bones.
> Let it be unto him as the garment which covereth him, and for a girdle wherewith he is girded continually.
> Let this be the reward of mine adversaries from the Lord, and of them that speak evil against my soul.
>
> Psalm 109:2-3, 17-20

This psalm describes those who enjoy creating lies. Their hatred causes them to speak words of ill will, harm, and destruction to the lives of others. They curse themselves with their own insidious motivations. If you tell them the truth, they don't want to hear it. They prefer to believe their lies and hold onto their ill will and invocations of harm.

Before you listen to and agree with any demeaning words, you had better find out the truth, because words of curse could come back upon your own life.

Words Of Blessing *And* Cursing?

But the tongue can no man tame; it is an unruly evil, full of deadly poison.

Therewith bless we God, even the Father; and therewith curse we men, which are made after the similitude of God.

Out of the same mouth proceedeth *blessing and cursing.* My brethren, these things ought not so to be.

Doth a fountain send forth at the same place sweet water and bitter?

Can the fig tree, my brethren, bear olive berries? either a vine, figs? so can no fountain both yield salt water and fresh.

James 3:8-12

God cannot bless those who curse others. A blessed person does not speak cursing or try to reduce someone to elevate himself. He has no desire to cut, wound, and inflict pain. A person who speaks curses is self-boasting; he sets up his own standards as truth, nullifies the Word of God, and, unfortunately, leads others into demonic deception.

The following prayer will help you to identify and remove words of curse that others have spoken over your life.

Father, I renounce my confidence in the flesh, for my

24

trust is in You. I will not fall prey to electioneering motivations.

In Jesus' Name, I command every demonic word of curse and every agreement with words of destruction to bow. I command them to release their holds on my life now. I mandate the words of curse, "Return to those who spoke you." Those words have no more life. By the power of Jesus' Blood, I command and decree all genetic and organizational curses are broken from me and my family.

I confess now that from my mouth will come only blessing and not cursing. With my tongue I bless You, Father, and give You all honor and glory. In Jesus' Name. Amen.

2
Break All Curses On Your Life

Have you already recognized causes of curse that have broken your communion with God and prevented you from moving in His consistent, perpetual blessing? Do you find that you must justify and vindicate yourself to others, because you know that curses stand against you? The question now is how do you handle a curse that is affecting your life? What do you do if there is someone who is cursing you?

Forgive The Person

We Wrestle Not Against Man

First, you must recognize that you are not wrestling against the flesh and blood of man. Your warfare is not with people; it is with your spiritual enemy, the devil. Paul wrote:

> For we wrestle not against flesh and blood, but against principalities, against powers, against the rulers of the darkness of this world, against spiritual wickedness in high places.
>
> Ephesians 6:12

Realize that you are in a "word warfare," not a "person warfare." You are not dealing with people. While you might be physically interacting with a parent, spouse, friend, or someone else, you must understand that you *really* are contending with the spiritual enemy who is working *through* them.

Don't try to fight the people who speak negative words over you. God has a law in place that will take care of them. You are to protect *yourself*, and let God do the rest.

> Our soul is escaped as a bird out of the snare of the
> fowlers: the snare is broken, and we are escaped.
> Our help is in the name of the Lord, who made
> heaven and earth.
>
> Psalm 124:7-8

God does deliver His people!

Judge Every Person As Dead In Christ
You need to judge everyone as dead in Christ. How?

> *For the love of Christ constraineth us; because we thus
> judge, that if one died for all, then were all dead:*
> And that he died for all, that they which live should
> not henceforth live unto themselves, but unto him which
> died for them, and rose again.
> Wherefore henceforth know we no man after the
> flesh: yea, though we have known Christ after the flesh,
> yet now henceforth know we him no more.
>
> 2 Corinthians 5:14-16

You need to judge that when Jesus died, He died with *every*
man in Him. As a result, everyone is dead in Christ. Whether
saved or unsaved, Jesus died for all men. That is the love of God,
and He calls *us* to love *all* men—even those who now curse us.
You must see all people with God's eyes of love. This
understanding will keep your heart tender and sensitive in
your relationships. Otherwise, you will become hardened and
calloused not only to other people, but to God.

Forgive In Jesus' Person And Name
You must forgive the person who cursed you, not because
you are strong or big enough, but because you understand the
enemy's plan. Realize that man in and of himself does not know

what he is doing. Recall what Stephen did when men rushed at him and "gnashed on him with their teeth" to kill him:

> And he kneeled down, and cried with a loud voice, Lord, lay not this sin to their charge....
>
> Acts 7:60

Stephen echoed Jesus' words as He hung on the cross:

> ...Father, forgive them; for they know not what they do....
>
> Luke 23:34

It will help you to remember that people don't recognize the influences under which they operate. They are like blind sheep, not understanding what is happening, but simply following blind shepherds. Paul wrote:

> To whom ye forgive any thing, I forgive also: for if I forgave any thing, to whom I forgave it, for your sakes forgave I it in the person of Christ;
> *Lest Satan should get an advantage of us: for we are not ignorant of his devices.*
>
> 2 Corinthians 2:10-11

> Follow peace with all men, and holiness, without which no man shall see the Lord:
> Looking diligently lest any man fail of the grace of God; *lest any root of bitterness springing up trouble you, and thereby many be defiled.*
>
> Hebrews 12:14-15

What does Paul mean in these two passages of Scripture? If you harbor bitterness and allow it to take root in your life, it will influence you and other people around you. You see, if people don't know how to contend with bitter words, they, too, become embittered when they listen to people negatively speak about others. On the other hand, if you forgive, your forgiveness will create a peace and a freedom in your environment.

Understand that you don't forgive in your great, gracious ability to forgive. You forgive the person in the Name of Jesus by faith. Jesus has forgiven you; and through the power of His cleansing Blood, you forgive others, "lest Satan should get an advantage" over you.

What happens if Satan gets an advantage? Curses come. Remember, a curse without an advantage (causeless) shall not come; but given an advantage, it comes. A curse does not get the advantage if you remain under the Blood of Jesus and obediently forgive others.

When someone hurts us, our flesh would like "an eye for an eye, and a tooth for a tooth" (Matthew 5:38). However, Jesus taught us to forgive, forbear, and be long-suffering with every person around us. We are not to judge, harbor ill will, accuse, condemn or think on evil accusations.

Forgive And Do Not Judge

Matthew recorded Jesus' words about the law of forgiveness in Chapter 18 verses 21-35. Here, Jesus told a sobering story about a servant who pleaded with his king to forgive a debt the servant owed. The king had compassion on the servant and agreed. Later, however, that servant refused to forgive another man's debt. When the king discovered this servant's double standard, he reinstated the servant's debt and threw him "to the tormentors." Jesus warned us:

> So likewise shall my heavenly Father do also unto you, if ye from your hearts forgive not every one his brother their trespasses.
>
> Matthew 18:35

You see, you are in a dangerous position if you don't forgive when a curse is spoken against you. If you refuse to forgive others, you will live in torment, and God will not forgive you. Jesus also said:

> For if ye forgive men their trespasses, your heavenly Father will also forgive you:
> But if ye forgive not men their trespasses, neither will your Father forgive your trespasses.
>
> Matthew 6:14-15

> Judge not, and ye shall not be judged: condemn not, and ye shall not be condemned: forgive, and ye shall be forgiven.
>
> Luke 6:37

Here, not only did Jesus teach us to forgive, but He instructed us not to judge others. Otherwise, He will judge us. Paul reiterated this in his letter to the Romans:

> Therefore thou art inexcusable, O man, whosoever thou art that judgest: for wherein thou judgest another, thou condemnest thyself; *for thou that judgest doest the same things.*
>
> Romans 2:1

It is likely that someone who judges another individual is guilty of the same behavior that he is judging. You bring curse upon yourself when you judge others and refuse to forgive.

Repent For Your Own Evil Words

If someone has mistreated, abused, or cursed you, probably you, in turn, have judged and spoken negatively about the one who unjustly attacked you. This is very common, but dangerous. Do not fall into the same trap that your accuser is in. If you have done nothing to justify mistreatment, the devil would love to tempt you to fall by responding wrongly.

If you have done this, take the sword—the Word of God—and command yourself to be free from your own words; otherwise they will fall back upon your own head. (We will study this in detail later.) Then, repent for the evil words you have spoken about the other person. Recognize that unless you repent, you will eat your own words and cause your own death. Remember the verse we studied earlier:

> Death and life are in the power of the tongue: and they that love it shall eat the fruit thereof.
>
> Proverbs 18:21

Go to those to whom or about whom you have spoken evil words, and apologize to them. Decide that you never again will speak evil of anyone, regardless of any circumstances. Ask others to refrain from doing so in your presence. John wrote:

> If we confess our sins, he is faithful and just to forgive us our sins, and to cleanse us from all unrighteousness.
>
> 1 John 1:9

The way you repent is to hold fast your profession. You see, repentance is not merely feeling sorrow and remorse for your sin. It is also *turning* from that sin. This means simply that you don't do it anymore. Instead, you obey the Word. When you do this, God cleanses you from your sin:

> But if we walk in the light, as he is in the light, we have fellowship one with another, and the blood of Jesus Christ his Son cleanseth us from all sin.
>
> 1 John 1:7

Break The Curse

We have discussed that you must repent and forgive the

person, recognizing that he is not the *cause;* the curse simply is coming *through him from the enemy.* Now, you must break the power of the words of curse. How can you do this?

Three biblical actions can break the power of curses: the blood sacrifice, intercession, and action on God's Word.

Blood Stops The Curse

Let's consider the example of David:

> *And Satan stood up against Israel,* and provoked David to number Israel.
>
> 1 Chronicles 21:1

Do you realize that, so he can stand against you today, Satan may have provoked your great-grandfather to stand against the kingdom of God? Why? It could be because Satan knew the purpose you were to have in this generation. If you have had a hellish experience in coming to radical obedience and servitude to the Lord, it could be because Satan took action against you through your forefathers.

Continuing in 1 Chronicles 21, we read:

> And David said to Joab and to the rulers of the people, Go, number Israel from Beer-sheba even to Dan; and bring the number of them to me, that I may know it.
>
> And Joab answered, The Lord make his people an hundred times so many more as they be: but, my lord the king, are they not all my lord's servants? why then doth my lord require this thing? why will he be a cause of trespass to Israel?
>
> 1 Chronicles 21:2-3

Remember, a curse has to come through someone who gives place to it. Satan knew that he would have access to the people of God, if he could entice David to sin. David yielded and disobeyed the Lord.

33

So the Lord sent pestilence upon Israel: and there fell of Israel seventy thousand men.

1 Chronicles 21:14

Look at the consequences, here. One man's sin caused 70,000 people to die!

And David said unto God, Is it not I that commanded the people to be numbered? even I it is that have sinned and done evil indeed; but as for these sheep, what have they done? let thine hand, I pray thee, O Lord my God, be on me, and on my father's house; but not on thy people, that they should be plagued.

1 Chronicles 21:17

As the story unfolded, God gave three options to David; and David chose the one of dealing directly with God. As He commanded, David went to Ornan.

And as David came to Ornan, Ornan looked and saw David, and went out of the threshingfloor, and bowed himself to David with his face to the ground.

Then David said to Ornan, Grant me the place of this threshingfloor, that I may build an altar therein unto the Lord: thou shalt grant it me for the full price: that the plague may be stayed from the people.

1 Chronicles 21:21-22

David understood the blood covenant. Because blood is the sure means of stopping curses, David wanted to shed the blood of an animal in sacrifice to the Lord. Today, the Blood of Jesus shed on the cross of Calvary, when appropriated in faith, permanently stops the curse of sin for us.

And Ornan said unto David, Take it to thee, and let my lord the king do that which is good in his eyes: lo, I

give thee the oxen also for burnt offerings, and the
threshing instruments for wood, and the wheat for the
meat offering; I give it all.

1 Chronicles 21:23

This is very important. Please understand what this verse
means. Ornan didn't want David to bear the responsibility of
his own curse. We see the same problem today: many well-
intentioned individuals don't want others to bear the
responsibility of breaking curses for themselves. Many people
ask others, "Would you do it for me?" No! That's not how you
break the curse. Here, we see that David understood he needed
to do it *himself.*

And king David said to Ornan, Nay; but I will verily
buy it for the full price: for I will not take that which is
thine for the Lord, nor offer burnt offerings without cost.
So David gave to Ornan for the place six hundred
shekels of gold by weight.
And David built there an altar unto the Lord, and
offered burnt offerings and peace offerings, and called
upon the Lord; and he answered him from heaven by fire
upon the altar of burnt offering.
And the Lord commanded the angel; and he put up
his sword again into the sheath thereof.

1 Chronicles 21:24-27

David shed the blood, and God intervened. One way out of
the curse is by the declaration of blood.

Intercession Stops The Curse
The next way out of the curse is by intercession. In Numbers
14, we read that Moses interceded in the wilderness and stopped
the children of Israel's curse from passing onto their children.
Remember, in the previous chapter (13), Moses had sent 12
men "to spy out the land of Canaan" (verse 17). Instead of

believing the good report of Caleb and Joshua, the people accepted the other ten spies' evil reports. Therefore, God could not allow the Children of Israel into the Promised Land.

And the Lord said unto Moses, How long will this people provoke me? and how long will it be ere they believe me, for all the signs which I have shewed among them?

I will smite them with the pestilence, and disinherit them, and will make of thee a greater nation and mightier than they.

Numbers 14:11-12

God was about to destroy the entire race, including the children, so out of Moses would come a new generation which would enter and inherit the Promised Land. Remember, the curse has the right to go to all generations. So, God had already decided to stop the curse by killing this cursed people. However, Moses stood in the gap to intercede for the nation of Israel.

And Moses said unto the Lord, Then the Egyptians shall hear it, (for thou broughtest up this people in thy might from among them;)

And they will tell it to the inhabitants of this land: for they have heard that thou Lord art among this people, that thou Lord art seen face to face, and that thy cloud standeth over them, and that thou goest before them, by day time in a pillar of a cloud, and in a pillar of fire by night.

Now if thou shalt kill all this people as one man, then the nations which have heard the fame of thee will speak, saying,

Because the Lord was not able to bring this people into the land which he sware unto them, therefore he hath slain them in the wilderness.

And now, I beseech thee, let the power of my Lord be

great, according as thou hast spoken, saying,

The Lord is longsuffering, and of great mercy, forgiving iniquity and transgression, and *by no means clearing the guilty, visiting the iniquity of the fathers upon the children unto the third and fourth generation.*

Pardon, I beseech thee, the iniquity of this people according unto the greatness of thy mercy, and as thou hast forgiven this people, from Egypt even until now.

And the Lord said, I have pardoned according to thy word.

Numbers 14:13-20

Cursed people cannot intercede for themselves, and God cannot use a cursed individual to bring deliverance to someone else. Only the Spirit of God can intercede for a cursed people. Because Moses, under the power of the Holy Spirit, interceded—taking upon himself the deliverance of other people—the curse stopped right there and did not confer to the children. The next generation operated under Moses' commandment and was radically obedient. They broke the curse of their forefathers and inherited the Promised Land.

Action On God's Word Stops The Curse

We have seen that blood and intercession reverse the curse. Action on God's Word also has this power. Such is the biblical example of Rahab the harlot. We read her story in the book of Joshua, chapter two.

Rahab was a Canaanite—a woman from the cursed people who had descended from Canaan and Ham. (Remember, earlier we studied the Canaanites' generational curse of sexual perversion. It is no surprise that this Canaanite woman was a prostitute.) As the Israelites sought the Promised Land, God ordered them to kill all the Canaanites. Rahab lived in the city of Jericho in the territory of the Canaanites. She and her household were about to die.

One night, Joshua sent two spies to investigate the Promised

Land. However, when the king of Jericho searched for the spies, Rahab the harlot hid them on the roof of her house. (Because they were on the roof as spies proved that they were not stepping into sexual immorality with the harlot. They did not engage in activity with a cursed person whom they were about to kill.)

> And before they were laid down, she [Rahab] came up unto them upon the roof;
> And she said unto the men, I know that the Lord hath given you the land, and that your terror is fallen upon us, and that all the inhabitants of the land faint because of you.
> For we have heard how the Lord dried up the water of the Red sea for you, when ye came out of Egypt; and what ye did unto the two kings of the Amorites, that were on the other side Jordan, Sihon and Og, whom ye utterly destroyed.
> And as soon as we had heard these things, our hearts did melt, neither did there remain any more courage in any man, because of you: *for the Lord your God, he is God in heaven above, and in earth beneath.*
>
> Joshua 2:8-11

Rahab, a cursed woman, had confessed Jehovah as the supreme King, the Lord of all! Deuteronomy says:

> Know therefore that the Lord thy God, he is God, the faithful God, which keepeth covenant and mercy with them that love him and keep his commandments to a thousand generations.
>
> Deuteronomy 7:9

Here was a woman under the curse. She and her family were only a few days away from annihilation and utter destruction. Yet, Rahab declared that the Lord had blessed the nation of

Israel and that He "is God in heaven above, and in earth beneath." How did God respond?

The second chapter of Joshua tells the rest of Rahab's story: as the spies commanded, she put the scarlet thread in her window. Then, when the Israelites destroyed Jericho, Rahab and all her family were the only ones allowed to live. Later, she married a Jew and conceived a son, Boaz. Boaz married Ruth; their son Obed had a son named Jesse. Jesse's son, David, was in the lineage of Jesus Christ!

It was not very likely that this Canaanite woman would ever come out of the generational curse against her nation, but her heart was right with God. The God who keeps His covenant to a thousand generations stepped in and kept covenant with her. Action on God's Word reversed the curse for this one who was full of sin—a Canaanite destined to die. She acted in faith, honoring God, and the curse was broken.

What about you? It does not matter how cursed your environment may be. If you obey God's Word and act in faith, your covenant-keeping God will induce blessing to one thousand generations after you! If a cursed prostitute can get her heart right, stop the great open door of sexual perversion, see God honor her faith, and put Jesus in her lineage, think what God will do for *you* when you reverse the curse in your life! When one person acts according to the Word of God, the spirit of the enemy is broken.

How Can You Act On The Word?

The Word Of God Is Sharp And Powerful
The Word of God has power to sever and penetrate the spirit and soul. It traces out and passes judgment on every word or thought that we conceive.

> For the word of God is quick, and powerful, and sharper than any twoedged sword, piercing even to the dividing asunder of soul and spirit, and of the joints and

marrow, and is a discerner of the thoughts and intents of the heart.

Neither is there any creature that is not manifest in his sight: but all things are naked and opened unto the eyes of him with whom we have to do.

Hebrews 4:12-13

No matter how sharp a negative word is, the Word of God is sharper. It's like comparing a blunt instrument to a laser beam. The sharpest words anyone can say fail in comparison with the excellent cutting power of the Word of God. However, God's Word cuts to liberate, not destroy. It removes from a person the instruction of ill will and invocation of harm.

Take the sharp two-edged sword of the Word to eradicate the negative words and malicious intent of others in your life. The Word of God cuts deeply to the core to reveal the intentions behind words, not merely the outward sentence structure. When the Word of God becomes the standard of excellence in your life, it strips naked every word, activity, thought, intention, and motivation. It exposes that which was hidden. When this happens, you no longer need to vindicate, justify, or defend yourself.

Command The Words Of Curse To Break

Take the powerful Word of God's blessings, and command the words of curse to be broken. Eradicate the power of the curse's negativity that came from those evil words. Continually, pray the Word of God over your life:

No weapon that is formed against thee shall prosper; and *every tongue that shall rise against thee in judgment thou shalt condemn.* This is the heritage of the servants of the Lord, and their righteousness is of me, saith the Lord.

Isaiah 54:17

The word *condemn* in this verse does not mean "to send it to

Hell." It means "to deem it unfit for habitation," as when an inspector condemns a building and allows no one to live there. Declare this:

> I command condemnation to all negative weapons formed against me. I refuse negative words of judgment, ridicule, and prejudice. These have no right to inhabit my life. I command these words and every judgmental tongue raised against me to be powerless. I command these evil words to be void of life and condemned so nothing can live in them. In Jesus' Name. Amen.

When you declared that just now, what did you do? By standing on the Word of God, you have freed yourself through the Blood of Jesus. You have removed the influence of evil words on your life and those around you. You have raised the shield of faith, which gives you the advantage against curses.

As you stand on the Word, you are not confused or disoriented, for God is not the author of confusion. When you stand on the Word, you are not bowed down to compromise or deceit. You don't require the praises of men to feel significant. You walk after and serve the King of Glory, and His rewards are enough for you.

Watch The Words You Speak

Although we will discuss this in further detail in a later chapter, you must understand that to break the curses in your life, you need to watch your own words. Be sure that everything you say lines up with the Word of God. Otherwise, you will bring curses upon yourself.

> So they shall make their own tongue to fall upon themselves: all that see them shall flee away.
> Psalm 64:8

The book of Proverbs gives us many guidelines for guarding

the words that proceed out of our mouths.

Put away from thee a froward mouth, and perverse lips put far from thee.

Proverbs 4:24

There is that speaketh like the piercings of a sword: but the tongue of the wise is health.
The lip of truth shall be established for ever: but a lying tongue is but for a moment.

Proverbs 12:18-19

A man shall eat good by the fruit of his mouth: but the soul of the transgressors shall eat violence.
He that keepeth his mouth keepeth his life: but he that openeth wide his lips shall have destruction.

Proverbs 13:2-3

He that hath knowledge spareth his words: and a man of understanding is of an excellent spirit.
Even a fool, when he holdeth his peace, is counted wise: and he that shutteth his lips is esteemed a man of understanding.

Proverbs 17:27-28

What Is Your Response?

It doesn't matter how bad you are. It doesn't matter how cursed your family line has been. It doesn't matter what you have faced: insanity, financial impoverishment, economic destruction, business failure, or broken relationships. It doesn't matter how bad your life has been. Only one thing matters: what is your response? Are you willing to appropriate the power of the Blood of Christ? Will you act on God's Word? Are you willing to step into the intercessory line to break the conveyance of curse, so God can move through you for a thousand generations?

It takes only one person to act on and obey God's Word. In my family, it was known that divorce was rampant. I was the one who broke that curse. Mental insanity was strong in our history. It broke and ended in me. Economic destruction had been in my forefathers' lives until it was broken in me. I am not cursed.

An action of obedience seals the covenant and induces blessing after blessing. What can the enemy ever do to come against you from that point forward? I believe it's time to break the genetic and organizational curses that have so affected you. You need to appropriate the Blood of Jesus. As we studied, David understood that he could not make a cheap sacrifice. The sacrifice to liberate your life was not cheap. It was Jesus Who stopped the curse against you and me. That Blood has already dealt the death blow to the power of sin and has given us the right of freedom and forgiveness.

We need to stand in the gap to intercede for the oppressed— those who don't recognize the power that affects them. We need to stop living under unseen, unknown curses. Act now. Obey God's Word to remove the curses in your life. Pray this as a declaration of your faith, today:

> Father, I thank You for the power of Your Word that is sharper than any two-edged sword. I judge all men dead in Christ, washed by the power of the Blood. I bless those who curse me and invoke good will upon their lives. I speak words of forgiveness and cleansing for them, not words of judgment. I pray that they can walk in fellowship with You.
>
> Father, I thank You that the Blood of Jesus has cleansed me of all sin. I confess that with my words, I have not walked in the counsel of Your wisdom, but have been negative, critical, judgmental, and demeaning.
>
> Father God, You love me so much that You sacrificed Your Son, Jesus. He shed His Blood and became the

curse for me. I repent of my sinful activities and declare that His Blood has washed the stain of sin from my life.

Father, I stand in the gap and make intercession for all those who live under the oppression of curses. Intercessor, mighty Spirit of God, rise up and cause them to know what You have called them to, and reverse the curses that bind them. Release them from their bondages. Loose the family of the living God.

Father, I stand in the power of Your Word. I bow to You. I will obey You. I will not bow to lies and deceptions again. I bow to the communion of Your Spirit that puts an end to the curse. Help me to speak only that which lines up with Your Word. I love You with all my heart. You are Lord of my life. In Jesus' Name. Amen.

3
Correct Your Self-Cursed Thinking

Those who do not study and understand all the laws and principles of God's Word snare themselves by their own misconceptions. Many people assume that when they obey God in one area, He will correct all areas of their lives. For example, when a person attends church regularly, he thinks God will see and straighten out everything in his life. Or, he says, "I prayed about it," and assumes that everything will work out because of what he has contributed to it. Ultimately, he can become embittered against God or people, because he doesn't understand God's laws that govern success in every area of life.

In other words, showing up in a building on Sunday and listening to the Word of God for 35 minutes doesn't mean that God will intervene in your life. Neither does praying about a need mean that you will receive an instant answer from the Lord. You see, to reap the blessings God promises in the Bible, you must understand that His laws require your participation with and obedience to His entire Word. *God's blessings are there for you; but you will not enjoy them unless you first know how His Word says to appropriate blessings, and then you do it.*

See Past The Words
To Recognize The Motives

Out Of The Abundance Of The Heart
You cannot take one law out of context from the Word and expect God to bless you. You must understand Scriptures within their contexts. Only a partial knowledge of the Word of God can hurt you.

For example, the Bible tells us that out of the abundance of the heart the mouth speaks. No one can vary, augment, or change this law. There is a relationship between the heart and spoken words. So, we believe that the words we hear from others actually reflect what is in their hearts. However, people can deceive us with their words when the true motives of their hearts are diametrically different. After we discover their true motives, we are likely to distrust people, and it negatively affects our lives. So, we need to discern the difference between the motives of the heart and the words of man. We need the blessing of wisdom and understanding so we *clearly* can see other people's true motives, regardless of their words or actions.

Now, let's look at what Jesus said about this law in its context, so we can understand it fully:

> Either make the tree good, and his fruit good; or else make the tree corrupt, and his fruit corrupt: *for the tree is known by his fruit.*
>
> *O generation of vipers, how can ye, being evil, speak good things? for out of the abundance of the heart the mouth speaketh.*
>
> A good man out of the good treasure of the heart bringeth forth good things: and an evil man out of the evil treasure bringeth forth evil things.
>
> Matthew 12:33-35

These verses are clearly about the *fruit* of men's lives. We cannot merely hear others' words and expect them to reflect accurately what is in their hearts. No, we also must examine the fruit of their lives. If you fail to do this, you could come to the wrong conclusion about others' true thoughts and motives.

You see, our words produce fruit. Unless God supernaturally reveals it to you, you normally do not see the root of a person. However, you always can tell what he is by his fruit—by what is evident and multiplied in his life. You can tell a man by the visible results of his life.

As A Man Thinketh

Have you ever had people tell you, "Well, have a good day," and you knew that their hearts were not in those words? Or, have you heard others say, "I hope what you do succeeds"? Yet, you knew they really hoped that you would fail miserably, so they could feel better about their own lack of effort. Their words did not reflect their true motives. If you trust them according to their words, you will find yourself in trouble.

Let's examine another law about this found in Proverbs: as a man *thinketh* in his heart, so is he. *You always must remember that the* thoughts *of the man make him what he* really *is, not his words to you.* Don't let the outward appearances fool you. Curses can be in a man's heart (real); yet his words (outward) may appear to bless you. Often we presume that when someone says something, that's how it will be. However, not everything is as it is said; it really is according to the heart. Learn to recognize when someone appears to bless you with his words, yet is cursing you with his thoughts. To see the truth, you need to remove the clutter in your life.

Again, let's look at this Proverb about thinking in its context:

> Eat thou not the bread of *him that hath an evil eye,* [covetous, self-seeking gain] neither desire thou his dainty meats:
> *For as he thinketh in his heart, so is he:* Eat and drink, saith he to thee; but his heart is not with thee.
> The morsel which thou hast eaten shalt thou vomit up, and lose thy sweet words.
>
> Proverbs 23:6-8

In our spirits, we don't want to consider that a person may have an evil, covetous eye. We simply don't want to think that somebody could be leading us on. In a positive sense, we often quote part of the above passage: "For as he thinketh in his heart, so is he." However, when we read the verses in context, we see that the Word does not use this verse positively. These words describe a deception with a graphic outcome of embitterment. You see, you can spend time with someone who speaks sweet words and appears well-intentioned toward you; yet your relationship can be one sided. Everything you do with that person will come out of you, because he really has not committed his heart to you. To solve the problem, then, you must go back to the root and undo everything.

Let me give you an example. You enter a partnership with someone who has a covetous eye, whose objective is to get everything he can for himself with no regard for your life. However, you are not aware of his true motivations. His words are, "We are going into this together. I will put in 100%, and you put in 100%. The two of us are going to do very well together."

So, you jump into the partnership thinking these are sweet words of common effort to reach common objectives. As time passes, however, you finally realize that your partner's motivation was not for common benefit but for his own self-seeking gain. In the end, you not only must dissolve the partnership, but you must go back to its origin to loose yourself from the deceitfulness of his sweet words.

The book of Proverbs says:

> Wisdom is the principal thing; therefore get wisdom:
> and with all thy getting get understanding.
> Proverbs 4:7

If you don't have the wisdom of God in a relationship, words may appear sweet to you; but later you could need to eject everything you had ingested. You must learn to use the Word of God to test the heart motives within a relationship. If you don't, you will be either uncertain that you truly can trust anyone, or you will want to believe so much in people that you fail to listen to what people say or see what they do.

You must see past the clutter of words. Rid yourself of your own emotions that desperately want to believe in others, despite facts that point to the contrary. Many people ignore major character flaws in others, because they don't want to see and deal with them. They say, "Well, I just see the best in everyone."

Now, I will judge everyone as dead in Christ, but I only will trust to the level of a person's character development. For instance, if a Christian were about to take my car to California, I would be sure to check his driving record. He might say, "Why are you looking at my driving record? Don't you trust me?" Checking his record would have nothing to do with my trust that Jesus died for him. It simply would be to confirm whether I should trust his character and whether he is a responsible driver.

Let's say, for example, that a man has accepted Jesus; God has forgiven his sin and he shares the grace of salvation. Now, he is a loving person. In his past, however, he has six proven counts of child abuse against him. He says to me, "I would just love to drive your children across town to get ice cream today. I hope you're not judging me for my past."

My response would be, "No. I judge that you are dead in Christ, but your convictions give me reason to distrust you in this particular area. I don't believe it's a good idea to have you take my children for ice cream on the other side of town, when there is an ice cream shop right next door."

You might say, "That is not showing Christian love." No, I love the man, but I cannot trust him until he demonstrates trustworthiness in this area. That is using the standard of the Word of God to decide a matter excellently.

You must let your spirit be aware, not naive, of other people's motivations. Pay close attention to that "still small voice" of the Holy Spirit within you (1 Kings 19:12). Then, use the Word of God to judge and examine others' thoughts. The first step in doing this is to remove the clutter from your mind.

Remove The Clutter From Your Mind

Recognize The Power Of Self-Deception
Deception is the practice of believing something that is not

true and acting on it. The Bible says:

> There is a way that *seemeth right* unto a man, but the end thereof are the ways of death.
>
> Proverbs 16:25

> But be ye doers of the word, and not hearers only, *deceiving* your own selves.
>
> For if any be a hearer of the word, and not a doer, he is like unto a man beholding his natural face in a glass:
>
> For he beholdeth himself, and goeth his way, and straightway forgetteth what manner of man he was.
>
> James 1:22-24

Self-deception is a terrible curse in our lives, because by it we add agreement to our ignorance. We begin to act on the deception, thinking it is true. This lie that appears correct to us, then, begins to motivate us. Because we tell ourselves that we are walking in truth, we become defensive of our own ignorance. When this happens, we don't want to hear the *real* truth.

Did you ever vehemently defend what you believed, only to learn that you were wrong? That was a miserable, humbling experience, wasn't it? Then, when you had to humble yourself and admit you were wrong, you probably tried to avoid the people who were rightfully walking in the truth; you didn't want to face the embarrassment of your display of ignorance.

The pride of life never wants to admit personal responsibility for the error of action. However, if you let pride rule you, you will forsake your own salvation to associate with people of like bondage. You will separate yourself from the light, rather than confess that you are self-deceived. Confession is the only way you can return to the correct decision path to reach God's objectives for your life.

Choose the right decision path, so you can walk in the light of the Word of God. You see, the Bible clearly exposes your entire heart to prevent self-deception. Always be ready to turn away from personal deception in your thoughts and actions.

Self-deception will cause you to follow a course that simply is not true—no matter how much you want it to be true. *Sincerity does not determine validity.* You can be entirely sincere in your belief, but that doesn't make it valid. I know some extremely sincere, deceived people. There is no validity to what they believe, yet they believe it with all their hearts. *If you want to determine the validity of your sincerity, look at the fruit of your action.*

Don't Let The World Dominate Your Thinking
Paul wrote to the Romans:

> And be not conformed to this world: but be ye transformed by the renewing of your mind, that ye may prove [put to the test and see what is true] what is that good, and acceptable, and perfect, will of God.
>
> Romans 12:2

Today in the United States, a polarization of thought exists. Secular humanists try to pull our minds to conform to what the world dictates, instead of to the perfect will of God. Our society deceitfully snares us by exalting man's opinion above the truth. This clouds our ability to perceive the truth and diminishes our wisdom. A stripping process, then, must occur to free our minds of this humanistic clutter, so we can see truth.

Carefully Choose The Company You Keep
You seriously must consider the friendships you make. The company you keep will ultimately bind your soul—you will emulate them (strive to be like them) or you will imitate them (duplicate their lifestyle).

> Make no friendship with an angry man; and with a furious man thou shalt not go:
> Lest thou learn his ways, and get a snare to thy soul.
>
> Proverbs 22:24-25

A snare is a trap that captures you. Your soul will become captured by the company you keep. For example, if you spend time with someone who is angry with another person, you will pick up or borrow that attitude and also be angry.

The book of Proverbs says:

> Be not thou envious against evil men, neither desire to be with them.
> For their heart studieth destruction, and their lips talk of mischief.
>
> Proverbs 24:1-2

If you have friends who are bitter, prejudiced, judgmental, or covetous, the clutter of their negative traits will begin to affect you. If you spend time with an envious, backbiting person, who continually speaks evil reports, you will become like him. If you hang out with people who talk mostly about financial loss, your soul will be bound by economic disaster. If your conversations are always about marital misery, your soul will be bound in marital misery.

Your associations can snare your soul and become curses in your life. So, you are self-cursed by your friendships and the company you keep. You must loose yourself from this clutter. Renew your mind by the power of the Blood of Jesus and the wisdom of the Word of God.

At this point, I want to lead you in a prayer that will help you to clear the clutter from your mind. Pray this from your innermost being and allow the Holy Spirit to reveal to you specific areas where you need help:

> Father, I thank you for the power of the Blood of Jesus that forgives and forbears.
> I determine to have wisdom, and I ask for the ability to understand others, so I can rightly perceive motivations of the heart. I release from my life the hold of every word of mal-intent that I have received. I loose

every bitter, envious, and angry associate. I repent and turn from any areas of self-deception, now. I will not fashion myself after the patterns of this present age. Instead, I put myself in subjection to Your Word that will change me and renew my mind. In Jesus' Name. Amen.

Turn On The Light,
Then See What You Think

The entrance of thy words giveth light; it giveth understanding unto the simple.

Psalm 119:130

As you prayed just now, did people, situations, or conversations come to your mind? Your prayer turned on the light of God's truth in your mind. You received understanding simply from the few sentences you prayed. You may have seen relationships and associations. Perhaps you saw negative and bitter people. Maybe, you saw the binding of your soul; and as you prayed that simple prayer, it brought illumination to you.

To correct your thinking, you need to break the power of your past negative experiences, conditional learned behaviors, repetitive thoughts, and actions. How do you do this?

Base Your Decisions Upon The Standard
Of God's Word

The clutter in our minds comes from man's thoughts—our experiences and how we judge situations—not the truth of the Word of God. We must turn on the light of God's Word to illuminate our minds so we can see matters accurately; otherwise, we may impose curses upon ourselves. We find ourselves in negative situations and don't know how to escape. Then, we walk away with false imaginations, conformity to the world, wrong thoughts and judgments, bitterness, and anger. These have nothing to do with reality, but rather with our incorrect perceptions. This is how self-deception begins.

53

We must fearlessly let the Word set a correct standard to which we can compare our thoughts. Philippians says:

> For the rest, brethren, whatever is true, whatever is worthy of reverence and is honorable and seemly, whatever is just, whatever is pure, whatever is lovely and lovable, whatever is kind and winsome and gracious, if there is any virtue and excellence, if there is anything worthy of praise, think on and weigh and take account of these things—*fix your minds* on them.
>
> Philippians 4:8 (AMP)

Now, certain thoughts may be true, but not lovable. Certain reports about someone may be true, but not good. Certain situations may be true, but not worthy of praise. Certain people of great intellect may not be worthy of honor.

So, what are you to "fix" your mind on? How can you discern what is lovable, honorable, praiseworthy, and of good report? You must line up every thought and action with the Word of God. Screen them through the Bible. Thoughts may be true, but are they worthy of recognition; are they just; are they pure? Compare your every thought to the Word of God.

Accept God's Word As The *Only* Authority For Change

So, it's time to correct your thinking. How do you do this? You might say, "I can change my own mind to correct my thinking." No, you can't. It's proven in the Word.

> Then said Jesus to those Jews which believed on him, *If ye continue in my word,* then are ye my disciples indeed;
> And *ye shall know the truth,* and the truth shall make you free.
>
> John 8:31-32

Only when you stay in the Word of God will your thinking

begin to conform to the truth of God's standards. Then, your thoughts, words, actions, and fruits will begin to reflect your discipleship in Christ. This is how you become set free.

It's critical that teenagers study especially the Word in Psalms and Proverbs. For example, Proverbs 6:1-3 says:

> My son, if thou be surety for thy friend, if thou hast stricken thy hand with a stranger,
> Thou art snared with the words of thy mouth, thou art taken with the words of thy mouth.
> Do this now, my son, and deliver thyself, when thou art come into the hand of thy friend; go, humble thyself, and make sure thy friend.
>
> Proverbs 6:1-3

Imagine being 16 years old and knowing never to become a surety—a co-signer or guarantor. Do you realize how many cases would not be in the court system now, if everyone had refused to guarantee other people's debt? When that teenager is 25 years old and a relative asks him to be a co-signer on a car loan, how will he respond? "I'm sorry," he will say. "I have grown up on the Word of God, and the Word says not to enter into an agreement of suretyship."

Many of us don't understand the principles of the Word of God. So, we end up snaring ourselves—and our futures—because we want to be nice to people; we want to help somebody out. This is a curse, because *what we do in violation of the Word of God becomes a curse.* An incorrect, non-biblical relationship is a cursed relationship. No matter how much you desire good to come out of it, God cannot bless it.

Many of us are self-cursed because we don't think correctly and are afraid that someone will not like us. If your thinking isn't correct, everyone else will think for you, and their bondages will control you.

Basically, your mind is cluttered and corrupt until you renew it. The older you become and the more experiences you have, the more clutter builds up in your mind. To derive freedom, then, you must rightly decide matters according to the truth, and then continue in that truth. Jesus said:

> Sanctify them through thy truth: thy word is truth.
> John 17:17

> And ye shall know the truth, and the truth shall make you free.
> John 8:32

Only truth has the power to cleanse and liberate; and the Word of God is the only valid standard for absolute truth.

> Wherewithal shall a young man cleanse his way? by taking heed thereto according to thy word.
> Psalm 119:9

> Now ye are clean through the word which I have spoken unto you.
> John 15:3

> Seeing ye have purified your souls in obeying the truth through the Spirit unto unfeigned love of the brethren, see that ye love one another with a pure heart fervently.
> 1 Peter 1:22

How do you become clean? You diligently and consistently apply the Word of God. How do you free your soul? You take the truth and act on it. To get free, it takes a radical purification of the soul and a deep commitment to freedom.

Choose To Change

You must decide to change. It might not be an easy road, but the freedom that you gain will be well worth your effort.

Change Should First Face The Difficult Areas Of Life

When you choose to change, don't start with the path of least resistance. Choose the difficult areas that need changing. Whatever is necessary to eliminate from your life, whatever is necessary for change, make that your path of choice. *Don't ever choose the path of least resistance.* If you do, you'll have to go back to start over. Get at the root of what's wrong, and get your foundation right so you can grow properly from there. Jesus said first to bind the strong man (Matthew 12:29).

Paul wrote to the Romans:

> And that, knowing the time, that now it is high time to awake out of sleep: for now is our salvation nearer than when we believed.
> *The night is far spent, the day is at hand: let us therefore [choose to] cast off the works of darkness, and let us [choose to] put on the armour of light.*
>
> Romans 13:11-12

You don't have the time to build on faulty foundations, only to tear it all down to start over. Decide today to change where you need it most.

Now, let's look at the story of two sisters: Martha and Mary. Think about the choices each made.

> Now it came to pass, as they went, that he [Jesus] entered into a certain village: and a certain woman named Martha received him into her house.
> And she had a sister called *Mary,* which also *sat at Jesus' feet, and heard his word.*
> But *Martha was cumbered about much serving,* and came to him, and said, Lord, dost thou not care that my sister hath left me to serve alone? bid her therefore that she help me.

And Jesus answered and said unto her, Martha, Martha, thou art careful and troubled about many things: But one thing is needful: and *Mary hath chosen that good part, which shall not be taken away from her.*

Luke 10:38-42

What should you do to choose the "good part"? What do you need to remove from your life that is troubling you and keeping you from sitting at the feet of Jesus to hear the Word? Make it your top priority to rid your life of those encumbering matters.

Break Up Your Fallow Ground

When you choose to change, you must identify resistance, stubbornness, self-opinions, and stagnant reasons. Simply because you have thought a certain way for years doesn't mean that it's right. *Longevity of ignorance doesn't turn it into truth; neither does sincerity nor commitment to it.* Begin to break up the areas in your life that are resistant, stubborn, and stagnant.

Sow to yourselves in righteousness, reap in mercy; *break up your fallow ground:* for it is time to seek the Lord, till he come and rain righteousness upon you.

Hosea 10:12

Fallow ground is soil that farmers have cultivated then allowed to remain idle during the growing season. When farmers break up fallow ground, they cut a fresh furrow in it for planting. To sow yourself in right relationship with God, you must cut a furrow through any hardened areas in your heart. You must break it up.

Circumcise yourselves to the Lord, and take away the foreskins of your heart...lest my fury come forth like fire, and burn that none can quench it, because of the evil of your doings.

Jeremiah 4:4

You cut through to plow in your *own* ground. Don't say, "God, if it's Your will, change me!" *You* must choose to change yourself. You can and should ask God to *reveal* to you areas where you need to change; but then it's up to you to repent and take steps to change in those areas.

> For thus saith the Lord to the men of Judah and Jerusalem, *Break up your fallow ground,* and sow not among thorns.
>
> Jeremiah 4:3

Break up the fallow ground of your heart. Deal with what's wrong in you first. Remember, Jesus said to remove the log from your own eye, and then you can see to remove the splinter from your brother's eye (Matthew 7:1-5).

Be Ruthless In Your Change

The only way to correct your thinking and remove self-curses is to deal ruthlessly with your soul by the Word of God. I cannot stress this enough. You must be ruthless—not with people—with your own thinking; and you must be consistent about it. We cannot deal with ourselves lightly. We must deal ruthlessly, violently. Now, I am not talking about self-abuse in a physical sense; but you must decide to penetrate your heart with the truth of the Word, and let it root out the evil seeds that would produce evil fruit. Otherwise, the blessing that God has designed for you will not be your portion. Instead, you will act in self-deceit, thinking you are on the right path. However, it will end in your destruction.

Sometimes when you start to deal ruthlessly with your own convictions, you may act differently. Do not allow any self-disappointments to affect the people around you. Purifying yourself is a radical process. You see, it is easy to become accustomed to the situational ethics of life—the status quo of accepted behavior. Then, when you start to purify your soul, you act contrary to the accepted norm. Sometimes, others perceive your behavior as insolent, arrogant, indifferent, or non-caring.

If you have been through internal changes to alter the way you think, you probably have had emotional instability during the transition. You were plowing through some rain-hardened, sun-parched areas of your life that no one had ever touched before. You were using the Word of God to plow through the hardness of your wrong motivations and thoughts to create a furrow for planting God's truth. The result—peace, blessings, contentment, and joy—however, always is well worth your effort!

Speak The Word Of God To Furrow

There are hundreds of Scriptures to use when you dig your furrow. Let those verses pull through your hardened conscience. Remember, as we studied earlier, the Word says that as a man thinks in his heart, so is he. How will you get your heart furrowed unless you are willing to change your thinking?

For example, you might say, "According to God's Word, I am healed: '...By whose stripes ye were healed'" (1 Peter 2:24).

Someone might point out, "Well, your body is still sick."

How do you respond to that? You say, "But the Word of God has not changed. I am healed!"

Speak the Word to confront your thinking. Say, "According to God's Word, Jesus Christ is Lord of my life. Therefore, I am saved!"

> But what saith it? The word is nigh thee, even in thy mouth, and in thy heart: that is, the word of faith, which we preach;
>
> That if thou shalt confess with thy mouth the Lord Jesus, and shalt believe in thine heart that God hath raised him from the dead, thou shalt be saved.
>
> For with the heart man believeth unto righteousness; and with the mouth confession is made unto salvation.
>
> Romans 10:8-10

The Word of God has not changed! If someone is judging you, start declaring:

> For thou, Lord, wilt bless the righteous; with favour wilt thou compass him as with a shield.
>
> Psalm 5:12

Remember, as we studied earlier, you stop the attacks of the enemy against you when you declare:

> No weapon that is formed against thee shall prosper; and every tongue that shall rise against thee in judgment thou shalt condemn. This is the heritage of the servants of the Lord, and their righteousness is of me, saith the Lord.
>
> Isaiah 54:17

Although your children may not appear blessed, declare:

> And all thy children shall be taught of the Lord; and great shall be the peace of thy children.
>
> Isaiah 54:13

The Word of God has not changed. If fear grips you, say:

> In righteousness shalt thou be established: thou shalt be far from oppression; for thou shalt not fear: and from terror; for it shall not come near thee.
>
> Isaiah 54:14

God wants you to prosper. Speak these words:

> Thus saith the Lord, thy Redeemer...I am the Lord thy God which teacheth thee to profit, which leadeth thee by the way that thou shouldest go.
>
> Isaiah 48:17

But my God shall supply all your need according to his riches in glory by Christ Jesus.

> Philippians 4:19

The Word of God gives power over habits.

I can do all things through Christ which strengtheneth me.

> Philippians 4:13

But let every man prove his own work, and then shall he have rejoicing in himself alone, and not in another.

> Galatians 6:4

For all that is in the world, the lust of the flesh, and the lust of the eyes, and the pride of life, is not of the Father, but is of the world.

And the world passeth away, and the lust thereof: but he that doeth the will of God abideth for ever.

> 1 John 2:16-17

Let the Word help you to do the will of God. Speak His Word of life over yourself. When you speak the Word from a renewed heart and mind, it produces life and blessing. Remember, as we studied earlier in Proverbs 18:20-21, the Bible promises that your words will come to pass. God will judge and hold us accountable for every word we speak! Jesus said:

But I say unto you, That every idle word that men shall speak, they shall give account thereof in the day of judgment.

For by thy words thou shalt be justified, and by thy words thou shalt be condemned.

> Matthew 12:36-37

We must plow to break up the fallow ground of our hearts

and plant the seeds of blessed words. Then, the fruit of God's blessing will be evident in our lives.

Know The "Rules Of The Word"

Would you prefer to know the game rules *before* you start playing, or be disqualified because you were playing under the wrong rules? That's what happens many times in life. We play by the rules of our experience instead of the true rules of God's Word, which govern every activity of life. Then, we wonder why circumstances don't work out for us. We wonder why we don't get the fruit we believed for. It's because we never furrowed, or dug in and broke up the fallow ground.

We can go to church; we can pray; we can ask God to change us; we can even read the Word of God; but until we actually use the Word to remove the clutter in our hearts and minds that are curses to us, we will not be free. Until we change our wrong attitudes, motivations, and behaviors, we will stay cursed. Even Christians who know the Word well suffer from self-curses, because they fail to take this vital step of change.

In 1987, after studying Joshua 1:8, I discovered the power of meditating on the Word of God. By meditating on leadership Scriptures, I knew a change would come. I needed a deep conviction of leadership not only for myself, but I knew that it would affect the lives of others around me. Now, I didn't like some of the Scriptures I meditated on, because they brought a tremendous sense of inadequacy and inferiority; they revealed the condition of my heart. However, those months of meditation changed my ministry. That time of furrowing in my heart, which lasted about 18 months, produced fruit that otherwise would not have been evident.

The only way you can destroy a self-curse is total commitment to breaking up the parched ground in your heart. You must focus on that topic until change results.

As you read the Word of God, let it sink deeply into your heart to reveal areas where you need to change. Honestly ask the Lord to reveal your areas of compromise, weakness, incorrect thinking, and wrong motivations. Be open to the Holy Spirit's conviction in every area of your life—even the innermost recesses of your being. Then, take immediate and ruthless steps to change in those areas that He shows you. To get started, pray this prayer now:

Father, I commit myself to the transformation of my soul through the truths of Your Word. As I break up my fallow ground, I allow the Holy Spirit to furrow in my heart. Reveal to me how I need to change.

I decree that I will not take the path of least resistance. Spirit of the Almighty God, help me as I anchor myself to the power of Your Word to bring change. I thank You that Your Word is the Standard of Truth for my life. In Jesus' Name. Amen.

4
Destroy The Self-Curse Of Hurt

Throughout life, the words and actions of others often hurt, disappoint and wound us. This personal pain is very real and can rob us of many precious years. If we don't seek healing, we will live in fear that someone will touch those wounds to cause us further suffering.

In this chapter, we will study what the Word of God says about the causes of emotional hurt; how one hurting person can multiply his pain into others and back to himself; and how to identify, isolate, insulate, and eradicate the hurt from oneself and others. God does not want any of His children to feel the destructive power of hurt.

> He healeth the broken in heart, and bindeth up their wounds.
>
> Psalm 147:3

Your heavenly Father wants to heal your broken heart right now. He wants to close your wounds. As you read this chapter, let Him minister to you through the power of the Holy Spirit.

Seeking God Prevents Hurt

Pastors Who Do Not Seek God Hurt Their Flocks

First, let's look at the hurt that results from not seeking God. This may come from a *pastor* who hurts God's people, because he relies on himself instead of seeking God's wisdom.

> Woe is me for my hurt! my wound is grievous: but I

said, Truly this is a grief, and I must bear it.

My tabernacle is spoiled, and all my cords are broken: my children are gone forth of me, and they are not: there is none to stretch forth my tent any more, and to set up my curtains.

For the *pastors* are become brutish, and have not sought the Lord: therefore they shall not prosper, and all their flocks shall be scattered.

Behold, the noise of the bruit is come, and a great commotion out of the north country, to make the cities of Judah desolate, and a den of dragons.

Jeremiah 10:19-22

This kind of hurt comes from a pastor who is not a praying person. If your pastor is seeking God, and his life is increasing and prospering, then you have a pastor who is walking in agreement with the purpose of God.

If, on the other hand, you have a pastor who does not seek God, he probably is lazy and says, "What's going to happen will happen. I can't do much about it. I can't pray effectively. I can't seek the Lord." Beware! This pastor can inflict hurt that will affect the Body of Christ. Why? It is because he does not seek the Lord, rise up early to pray, or spend significant time in the Word of God to understand it. Many just live to repeat their rituals and go from crisis to crisis.

People Who Do Not Seek God Hurt Themselves

There is also a hurt that occurs when an *individual* doesn't seek the Lord.

And the Lord hath sent unto you all his servants the prophets, rising early and sending them; but ye have not hearkened, nor inclined your ear to hear.

They said, Turn ye again now every one from his evil way, and from the evil of your doings, and dwell in the land that the Lord hath given unto you and to your

fathers for ever and ever:
And go not after other gods to serve them, and to
worship them, and provoke me not to anger with the
works of your hands; and I will do you no hurt.
Yet ye have not hearkened unto me, saith the Lord; that ye
might provoke me to anger with the works of your hands to
your own hurt.

Jeremiah 25:4-7

When a minister's or pastor's motivations are in line with
God's calling on his own life, he can speak truth into others'
lives, charging them not to stagnate, but to repent, turn from
sin, and return to God's purposes. Some people interpret this as
authoritarian and heavy-handed, saying, "The pastor is always
on me to do more for the church in Jesus' Name." Well, of course
he is. God calls pastors to provoke their flocks to good works.
This hurt is not coming from the minister, but from the
individuals who, although they hear the truth, stubbornly refuse
to change their lives. These types of responses are cries of self-
inflicted wounds.

These are people who have heard the Word of the Lord, yet
decide to go their own ways. They do not respond: "Yes, Lord,
I will obey You." Instead, they say, "Imagine the nerve of this
pastor, telling me that I have to win souls for Jesus, or that I have
to pray in the Holy Ghost, or that I have to lay hands on the sick,
or that I have to start believing God at a deeper level!" Because
they stubbornly refuse to change, they hurt themselves, then
blame others for their pain. These people do not realize that
they suffer hurt at their own hands.

Hurting People Multiply Pain

Gossip Hurts, But Love Covers And Corrects

Hatred stirreth up strifes: but love covereth all sins.
Proverbs 10:12

A hating person will expose the error of an individual to stir up discord because of what he sees, hears, or believes to be true. A gossip spreads and amplifies every little detail to others. However, a loving person will surround the individual in error until the healing process can begin and the ministry of God's grace can reach him.

Remember, spoken words can inflict a breach of relationship.

> He that covereth a transgression seeketh love; but he that repeateth a matter separateth very friends.
> Proverbs 17:9

While a person who operates in love is to cover the sin of others, he has an additional responsibility. *Love covers a multitude of sin and deals with that sin.* Love does not simply cover the sin and let the individual go about doing what he wants to do. No, love covers the sin, keeps the person protected from exposure to others, and then deals with that sin in his life.

> Open rebuke is better than secret love.
> Faithful are the wounds of a friend; but the kisses of an enemy are deceitful.
> Proverbs 27:5-6

You see, a person who, in biblical love, covers the sin of another not only takes on a covering responsibility with that person but also a rebuking responsibility. Those who love me expose to me the errors they perceive in my life—it could be my communication, activities, or another area. I find that I need those friends to keep me protected and to keep a good report around me; yet, in the intimacy of our relationship, they can talk frankly with me.

My wife is my best friend. If anything is in error in my life, such as discouragement, fear, or confusion, she quickly points it out to me. She doesn't say, "Well, Gary, that's all right. You are the pastor, so I can't say this to you." No, she protects me, surrounds me, and shares the Word of the Lord with me.

You may say, "Well, I don't like having my friends tell me what's wrong. When they do that, it hurts me." You must be careful. What you interpret as hurt could be the very wounds that God plans to use to begin your process of healing.

Gossips And Talebearers Harm Others

He that passeth by, and meddleth with strife belonging not to him, is like one that taketh a dog by the ears.

As a mad man who casteth firebrands, arrows, and death,

So is the man that deceiveth his neighbour, and saith, Am not I in sport?

Where no wood is, there the fire goeth out: so where there is no talebearer, the strife ceaseth.

As coals are to burning coals, and wood to fire; so is a contentious man to kindle strife.

The words of a talebearer are as wounds, and they go down into the innermost parts of the belly.

Burning lips and a wicked heart are like a potsherd covered with silver dross.

He that hateth dissembleth with his lips, and layeth up deceit within him;

When he speaketh fair, believe him not: for there are seven abominations in his heart.

Proverbs 26:17-25

When I was a young child, I made the mistake of grabbing a dog by its ears, wanting to ride him. Much to my surprise, the dog roared, turned around, and bit me. As a dog grabbed by its ears will bite you, so also will a talebearer gossip, spread evil reports, and inflict wounds in environments where he has no business.

You need to recognize and label those who cause division. Talebearers will take whatever is apparent, embellish it, and multiply it to keep the fires of gossip burning. Wounds can be deep when a talebearer spreads strife in situations where he has no business.

> The spirit of a man will sustain his infirmity; but a wounded spirit who can bear?
>
> Proverbs 18:14

To prevent talebearers' wounds in your life, you must identify people who meddle in others' affairs, and keep them at a great distance. Some people look for the smut in everything, and, if given the opportunity, will spread it to anyone who will listen.

We just read in Proverbs 26:23 about "burning lips" that can't wait to speak wicked words "and a wicked heart...like a potsherd covered with silver dross." This means a piece of broken pottery that looks beautiful on the outside, but is only clay on the inside. Verse 24 says, "He that hateth dissembleth with his lips." A person who hates always speaks words to separate, divide, and bring discord into others' lives. Verse 25 warns us to disbelieve the words of a talebearer, because we cannot trust the secret motivations of his heart.

Here, the Word says that where there is no wood, the fire goes out; and where there is no talebearer, the strife ceases. If people refuse to meddle in the affairs of others, the ill will from words exchanged between the others eventually will cease.

Evaluate the successful people around you. Do they sustain relationships, or are they covenant breakers? Are they surrounded by discord? Do they love the negativity of another's dilemma? Identify those who will wound you if you give them entrance, and those whose words will hurt you.

I pray every day of my life that God will deliver me from wicked and unreasonable men, for all men have not faith. I pray that the shield of faith will rise up around the Body of Christ, and that the words of talebearers and negative seeds sown by divisive people are brought down upon their own heads. I pray that those who desire the pure truths of God's Word will follow Him with all their hearts and that God will protect and deliver them from the hurt of talebearers' words.

Gossips And Talebearers Snare Themselves

When a person speaks against others, using negative words of hatred, bitterness, jealousy, envy, strife, pride, and self-seeking gain, he binds not only those he speaks against, but also himself. We read in Proverbs:

A fool's lips enter into contention, and his mouth calleth for strokes [stripes on his back].
A fool's mouth is his destruction, and his lips are the snare of his soul.

Proverbs 18:6-7

As we studied earlier, a snare is a trap that binds an unsuspecting prey. So, words that are spoken from the lips of a fool provide destruction for his own soul. His negative actions affect his mind, will, and emotions.

The words of a talebearer are as wounds, and they go down into the innermost parts of the belly.

Proverbs 18:8

Those who spread negative reports are fools whose words bind their own souls and inflict pain in their own and others' lives. Psalm 64 says:

Hear my voice, O God, in my prayer: preserve my life from fear of the enemy.
Hide me from the secret counsel of the wicked; from the insurrection of the workers of iniquity:
Who whet their tongue like a sword, and bend their bows to shoot their arrows, even bitter words:
That they may shoot in secret at the perfect: suddenly

71

do they shoot at him, and fear not.

They encourage themselves in an evil matter: they commune of laying snares privily; they say, Who shall see them?

They search out iniquities; they accomplish a diligent search: both the inward thought of every one of them, and the heart, is deep.

But God shall shoot at them with an arrow; suddenly shall they be wounded.

So they shall make their own tongue to fall upon themselves: all that see them shall flee away.

And all men shall fear, and shall declare the work of God; for they shall wisely consider of his doing.

Psalm 64:1-9

A person who speaks negative words about another individual is subject to having his own words fall back upon himself and thus wounding himself painfully. Also, the accuser of the brethren may come to him saying, "If that other person hadn't acted as he did, you wouldn't be in this mess." Remember the deceitfulness of sin? It causes people to believe others are at fault. No, the condition of a gossip's life results from being a negative, strife-dominated person; his words have fallen back upon his own head. His own foolish activities—not another's action—have caused the gossip's wounds. In fact, a person who sows strife always lives in pain, because he reaps his own words.

Frowardness is in his heart, he deviseth mischief continually; he soweth discord.

Therefore shall his calamity come suddenly; suddenly shall he be broken without remedy.

Proverbs 6:14-15

I have watched many people yield themselves to mischievous, talebearing thoughts and go on to sow discord among the brethren. I know that eventually their lives will come crashing down around them; and my heart breaks with the desire to heal them of these self-inflicted hurts. Calamity will come upon them from their own sin and foolishness. Then, they will say:

> For mine iniquities are gone over mine head: as an heavy burden they are too heavy for me.
> My wounds stink and are corrupt because of my foolishness.
> I am troubled; I am bowed down greatly; I go mourning all the day long.
>
> Psalm 38:4-6

These people will feel the self-inflicted wounds of their sins. Their own inadequacies will overcome them, and they will feel rejection, saying, "Everybody knows what a miserable person I am." You can avoid all this pain by refusing to gossip.

Maliciously Motivated People Curse Others

> They also that seek after my life lay snares for me: and they that seek my hurt speak mischievous things, and imagine deceits all the day long.
>
> Psalm 38:12

Are some people maliciously motivated? Absolutely! They are not necessarily gossips who inflict sin upon their own lives and wound themselves by their own foolishness. However, some people do intentionally devise hurt; they purpose destruction for the righteous and rejoice when something goes wrong. They love to say, "See, I told you. That person was out of order with God, and I was just waiting for it to destroy him."

These maliciously motivated people often target people who are not dwelling on hurts, mischief, or vicious gossip, but are keeping themselves from personal sin. Without warning, we can encounter people with malicious, deceitful desires to create lies intentionally to snare us.

Remember, the curse without an advantage cannot come (Proverbs 26:2). You must not give any armament to those malicious intentions. Those curses cannot come upon you, unless you give them an open door into your life. Protect yourself from others' evil desires by raising the shield of faith "and the sword of the Spirit, which is the word of God" against their curses:

> Above all, taking the shield of faith, wherewith ye shall be able to quench all the fiery darts of the wicked.
> And take the helmet of salvation, and the sword of the Spirit, which is the word of God.
>
> Ephesians 6:16-17

In chapter 35, the psalmist wrote:

> Let them be confounded and put to shame that seek after my soul: let them be turned back and brought to confusion that devise my hurt.
> Let them be ashamed and brought to confusion together that rejoice at mine hurt: let them be clothed with shame and dishonour that magnify themselves against me.
>
> Psalm 35:4, 26

Do Not Borrow Hurt

Sometimes borrowed hurt can occur in families. For example, let's say that two children, Johnny and Tommy, are playing together in a sandbox. They start to fight, and each boy goes home to his own mother. The next day, however, the boys have forgotten their hurts and are good friends again. They love each other, and they have a fun time playing together. All is forgiven and forgotten between them.

However, Johnny's and Tommy's mothers are at odds for years; and when the fathers pass each other on the street, they don't even speak. Why? The parents picked up borrowed hurt from their children. You see, hurt, like an infectious disease, will spread. It is critical that you don't allow its influence in your life.

Identify, Isolate, Insulate, And Eradicate Hurt

The process of becoming free from hurt involves identifying the hurt as sin, isolating and insulating it, and then eradicating it by the power of the Holy Spirit. When ministering to others or when dealing with your own hurts, you will need to follow these steps possibly in a different order at various times to remove the pain; and sometimes, you might need to repeat certain steps. However, to understand each part of the process, we will study each step separately here.

Identify Hurt As Sin

To be free, first you must see hurt as a snare to your soul— a sin. Am I really saying that it is a sin to feel and hold hurt when others do wrong to you? Yes! However, you must remember that the sin of hurt can be forgiven. You not only must forgive all the involved parties, but you need to be forgiven, also. I know this may not be easy to accept, but it is true.

Remember, 1 Corinthians 13:5 (AMP) says that love does not take account of a wrong suffered. Well, there it is: if you walk in love, you will not have an account of *any wrong suffered!*

Let's say that a man tells me that someone has wronged him, and now he feels hurt. If I reply, "Well, brother, you can be forgiven," what kind of reaction would I get?

"FORGIVEN?" the brother would ask, "I'm not the one who caused the hurt!" This is because most people don't recognize that to hold hurt is sin. Search the Scriptures. Where does the Bible give acceptable reasons for you to feel hurt and wounded in your spirit? The New Testament doesn't even discuss the hurts of relationships except to identify people who cause strife, and it says to avoid them. In fact, what people in church usually call "hurt" is not biblical at all. Typically, their hurt comes from talebearers and those in strife, because they are strife oriented.

When a hurting person comes to you, communicate the Word and wisdom of God peacefully.

> Who is a wise man and endued with knowledge among you? let him shew out of a good conversation his works with *meekness of wisdom.*
>
> James 3:13

You should not lambaste a hurting person, saying, "You had better repent because feeling hurt is sin." No, you need the "meekness of wisdom" to approach him with understanding, while not compromising the standards of truth in the Word.

Usually, the hurt was self-inflicted. You see, many people hurt because they haven't forgiven others. In our earlier example, Johnny's mother never forgave Tommy for what he did to her son. For years, it will keep Johnny's and Tommy's mothers from being friends. They feel hurt, because they refuse to forgive each other. The sad thing is that the mothers were not involved.

We need to forgive every person in the Name and person of Jesus. Remember, we studied earlier that if a person doesn't forgive from his heart, Jesus said he will be tormented. (See Matthew 18:28-35.) When we fail to release forgiveness to others, we become tormented and bound. Those hurts become snares with the power to bind our souls. This is *not* the will of God for man.

Isolate And Insulate The Hurt

You must isolate and insulate each hurt. I call this the "divide and conquer" method. Identify and separate the hurts to deal with them individually. Don't let hurts multiply, or they will deceive you. If you allow a hurt to breed in other areas, the person will feel discouraged about his *whole* life. Isolate each particular area. You do this as if you were to place that person in a medical isolation ward to contain the disease. You separate the person.

This is what you might say to someone who is hurting: "Let's do some evaluating. Now, this particular area is good in your life, and that is good. This is working, and that is functioning well for you. Now, let's isolate this one incident that apparently has hurt you. Let's encapsulate and insulate it to keep the infection from spreading. Let's keep it from influencing what is good in your life."

You see, someone with a lot of strife, division, and hurt may have several areas within himself that you need to isolate. Otherwise, the hurts will breed and multiply to the point that it will seem to him that everything has gone wrong, when in fact he has a lot of good areas in his life. He simply needs to isolate those areas of hurt and deal with them separately.

Incidentally, as we have discussed, this is true both within an individual's body and a corporate body, such as a church. If you don't isolate and minister to a strife-dominated, hurting person, you allow him to breed and influence others, like a disease. You must isolate those hurts so they will not contaminate others.

Insulation of hurt is a critical step. You must protect every area that needs healing from the conversations and opinions of others—even from the hurting person himself. Do not share your or others' pain with many people. Look to Jesus to heal it. Keep insulation around it, so it is not exposed to others. The spread of evil report ends at the point of insulation.

Eradicate The Hurt

After you have isolated and insulated it, then you need to eradicate the hurt. Maybe it's a spiritual bondage or a compromise. Maybe it's a cycle of behavior. No matter what the hurt is, the Holy Spirit, through prayer, can cut out and heal it; but you must give it all to Him. God is your *only* answer. The anointing binds up the broken heart. Nothing else can bring you relief from your pain.

"How Do You Spell *Relief?*"

A wounded person who seeks a remedy for his wounds will either turn to God for healing or to corruption. I believe that you will identify many people in this section. Too many look for relief in drugs, alcohol, and other destructive habits. The book of Proverbs says:

> My son, give me thine heart, and let thine eyes observe my ways.
> For a whore is a deep ditch; and a strange woman is a narrow pit.
> She also lieth in wait as for a prey, and increaseth the transgressors among men.
> Who hath woe? who hath sorrow? who hath contentions? who hath babbling? who hath wounds without cause? who hath redness of eyes?
> They that tarry long at the wine; they that go to seek mixed wine.
> Look not thou upon the wine when it is red, when it giveth his colour in the cup, when it moveth itself aright.
> At the last it biteth like a serpent, and stingeth like an adder.
> Thine eyes shall behold strange women, and thine heart shall utter perverse things.
> Yea, thou shalt be as he that lieth down in the midst of the sea, or as he that lieth upon the top of a mast.
> They have stricken me, shalt thou say, and I was not sick; they have beaten me, and I felt it not: when shall I awake? *I will seek it yet again.*
>
> Proverbs 23:26-35

When someone looks to further sin for comfort, he multiplies his sin and hurt. Instead of seeking healing of his self-inflicted hurt, he looks for relief in a sexual affair, drugs, alcohol, or some other abusive situation. Instead of a comfort, however, his sin becomes a yoke to him; yet, because of his self-deception, he will return to the bondage again and again.

"How do you spell *relief?*" J.E.S.U.S! It isn't liquor. It isn't cocaine or crack. It isn't an immoral sexual encounter or a fantasy relationship. Escape to sin is not the answer. Relief is allowing the grace and the power of the Lord Himself to deliver you from your bondage and pain.

These simple principles work in everyone's life. You can find freedom for yourself and for your family, right now, by turning to God. Are you feeling the pressure of betrayal? Do you feel hurt by other people's words of curse, negativity, division, strife, talebearing, and covenant breaking? God is ready to heal you, today! Respond to the anointing of the Holy Spirit, now.

What Is The Anointing For?

The anointing is the power of God. What does it do? The power of God breaks the yoke of repetitive, destructive actions—drug and alcohol abuse, adultery, and other debilitating sins.

> And it shall come to pass in that day, that his burden shall be taken away from off thy shoulder, and his yoke from off thy neck, and the *yoke* shall be destroyed because of the *anointing.*
>
> Isaiah 10:27

> The Spirit of the Lord God is upon me; because the Lord hath anointed me to preach good tidings unto the meek; he hath sent me to bind up the brokenhearted, to proclaim liberty to the captives, and the opening of the prison to them that are bound.
>
> Isaiah 61:1

There is a healing balm in Gilead (Jeremiah 51:8). My brother or sister, the anointing of the Holy Spirit is there with you now to heal all your hurts and self-inflicted wounds. It does not matter how divisive you may have been as a talebearer or what arguments you can make against those who have hurt you. Jesus wants to set you free, today. Turn to Him. Don't look for an escape in drugs, alcohol, or adulterous affairs. Don't be afraid that others will hurt you through your marriage, divorce, or abusive relationships. If someone maliciously abused you as a child, don't let that pain cripple your life one minute longer. The anointing is here to heal *all* the pain you have ever experienced. The power of the Holy Spirit wants to set you free from bondage! Rise up in His strength and peace to walk in His light, right now.

> Rejoice not against me, O mine enemy: *when I fall, I shall arise; when I sit in darkness, the Lord shall be a light unto me.*
>
> Micah 7:8

The enemy would love to see you stay down, unable to get back up again; but God has a better plan. When a person falls, he quickly gets back up, straightens himself out, acts as if nothing happened, and goes on with his life. That is how God wants to heal you. In your downfalls, He wants to empower you to get back up quickly to go on with your life. He wants the power of the Blood of Jesus to deliver you into a new freedom. God didn't design you to wallow in the tormenting oppression of your past. No! In His Word, here, He is telling you that if you are down, you shall rise again. The Lord will be a light to you.

It's time to turn around the curse in your life. It's time for the Word of the Lord to penetrate you. Put a demand on the anointing of God. Pray this prayer now to break any powers of oppression that have crippled and demeaned your life.

> Father, I turn to You as my answer. I seek only You, Lord. Forgive me for gossiping about others and for

holding on to hurt when others do wrong to me. Thank You for the anointing and the Blood of Jesus that breaks the yoke, cleanses, and forgives me.

Today, I forgive all those who have brought curses to my life. Thank You that I can reverse these curses of hurt in Jesus' Name. I send forth Your Word by the power of the Name of Jesus to remove the bondage of self-inflicted curses in my life. I command the crop of negative words to fail, and I declare those words reversed.

Holy Spirit of God, I thank You for the power of the anointing that brings freedom into my life now. In Jesus' Name. Amen.

5
Be Blessed,
Not Cursed Through Ignorance

What you don't know *will* hurt and cripple you, and reduce your life to an ash heap. When you lack knowledge and have a limited understanding, you permit curses to come upon you. The Prophet Hosea wrote:

> My people are destroyed for lack of knowledge...

Ignorance or partial knowledge of God's Word permits destruction, curse, oppression, calamities, and negative circumstances. The verse continues:

> ...because thou hast rejected knowledge...

Rejection is a decision. This means that you have rejected what you should have known. The teacher—the Holy Spirit—is in you, constantly bringing to your remembrance everything that Jesus said. When you don't listen to His voice, you reject the knowledge He has given to you. You must realize that this is not unintentional or accidental ignorance. *Ignorance is a decision.*

Does the Bible say that you will be excused from calamity, because you didn't know how to prevent it? Or, no one told you what you needed to know? No. Read the rest of this verse:

> ...I will also reject thee, that thou shalt be no priest to me: seeing thou hast forgotten the law of thy God, *I will also forget thy children.*

> Hosea 4:6

This is an interesting statement. *What you don't know about the Word of God will affect generations to come.* What you reject creates an atmosphere of curse that flows through you to other people. Conversely, what you do know and obey in God's Word will bring an atmosphere of blessing to your children and to those in your environment.

You have great authority to cause or to permit circumstances to happen. Curse can come through the enemy if you do not use that authority. You can let negative circumstances occur, or you can stop them. What you let happen will either stop destruction or enable destruction. It will either engage the purpose of God or disengage the purpose of God. We permit many undesired circumstances in our lives, because we do not give advantage to the knowledge of God's Word. Some people call this the "Permissive Will of God." However, this is a misnomer; it is not God, but the individual, who permits the evil circumstances. God does not will or choose evil for our lives. No! *Through our permission—we let the curse of ignorance, in its many forms, rule and destroy our lives.*

What Does *Let* Mean?

The word *let* has two distinct meanings. One is "to cause" and the other is "to permit." You need to understand these meanings. Otherwise you will miss the point of how to remove the curse that results from ignorance. To *cause* something, you must take a course of action to make it happen. On the other hand, to *permit* something, you yield without resistance, and it happens by default.

For example, if I say, *"Let's* have dinner," when no one has prepared a meal, I will need to *cause* someone to prepare it. My idea of having dinner will not become a reality unless someone causes it to happen.

On the other hand, *let* also can mean "to permit." A historian could say that the Americans *let* the Japanese invade Pearl Harbor. They permitted destruction because of unpreparedness.

To *permit* means "not to resist an action for or against." We can permit good and bad. Again, understand that when the enemy rules our circumstances, this is not the Permissive Will of God. It is man granting permission—without resistance—to the enemy to act. Many of us *let* the enemy have rule in our lives, not because we invited him but because we permitted him— often unknowingly. Usually, then, we blame God for the challenges we face; we label them as His will, when actually *we permitted the problems* by our lack of restraint.

To *cause* means "action which produces results." For example, to slow down your car you *let* your foot off the gas pedal. Does the car slow down by itself? No, you cause it to slow down. If someone in the car says, "Let's slow down," you do not simply say, "All right. I'll *permit* that to happen." No, you must *cause* it to happen.

In both definitions of *let*, we see that the person who either permits or causes is the authority. We can either use or fail to use that authority to make certain events happen or to prevent them. Every Scripture that says "you let," means that you are accountable and responsible for the outcome of that sentence. The ball is in your court. When you *let*, it is as if God were, at that point, out of the picture. He already has set the course of action. Now, man is accountable and responsible for what happens.

Who Backs Up The Authority, And How?

God—Who is and has all authority—gave to man certain realms of authority which, when properly used, produce God's results. We see this in Genesis:

> And God said, *Let* us make man in our image, after our likeness: and *let them have dominion* over the fish of the sea, and over the fowl of the air, and over the cattle, and over all the earth, and over every creeping thing that creepeth upon the earth.
>
> Genesis 1:26

God took a cause initiative. He took the action necessary to create man. Then, He *let* man have authority, rule, and dominion over the earth. Consider authority—the legal right to use power. *The* Authority, God, must back all authority.

Paul said to the Romans:

> *Let* every soul be subject unto the higher powers. For there is no power but of God: the powers that be are ordained of God.
>
> Whosoever therefore resisteth the power, resisteth the ordinance of God: and they that resist shall receive to themselves damnation.
>
> Romans 13:1-2

Does this *let* mean "to cause" or "to permit"? You don't *cause* the authority to have influence in your life; you *permit* that authority to have the influence. So, you permit your soul—your mind, will, and emotions—to come into subjection. You say, "That authority is of God, and I arrange myself under it. If I don't, I would be giving the one in authority the right to inflict a just penalty upon me." The authority figure is not wrong, if he penalizes you for disobedience. No, your penalty occurs because of your ignorance—you *let* yourself step into an area of penalization. Therefore, to your own detriment, you decided not to set yourself under authority.

For example, when my daughter, Laurie, was a teenager, she was penalized $100 for driving 77 miles per hour in a 55-mile-per-hour zone. Did this driver submit herself to the speed laws? No. Did the magistrate who imposed the fine have the authority to do so? Yes. Now, do I try to fix the speeding ticket? Do I call my friend who is the administrator in the local police department to say, "I'm the father of this particular individual"? No! That would be siding with the curse, and I would be permitting destruction in my life, home, and family. The $100 fine is a minor penalty compared to my letting the enemy have the advantage in my family.

In life, if you don't know the spiritual laws governing each circumstance, you can multiply your destruction unknowingly. How? By choosing a convenient alternative to avoid something that appears negative, you can create greater destruction. For example, instead of understanding the benefits of certain consequences, many parents try to fix their children's problems. In ignorance, they step into and multiply curses in their families; they fail to recognize that when they give advantage to the enemy's curse, they unleash destruction into their children's lives. Instead, parents need to understand that God places His instruments of authority into their children's lives, and the children need to pay proper penalties for their own good.

No authority exists but that which comes from God. If you resist authority, you open the door to curses. Do you have the right to say to the police officer who pulls you over for speeding, "I don't like this ticket. Don't give it to me"? No! You *let* it happen. First, you *caused* yourself to speed. Your action of disregarding the speed limit has consequences: a ticket and fine. You *permitted* the ticket and fine to be assessed to you when you chose to speed.

Now, most of us don't want to accept the responsibility of our actions and learn the truth about self-imposed curses. However, when I talked with my daughter and told her that I temporarily was removing her driver's license, she absolutely submitted to authority. "Whatever you want to do," she said, "is fine with me. I understand completely that I am accountable and responsible for my actions." She called the magistrate court and paid the fine before the bill came in the mail. Then, she called the police station to sign up for a defensive driving class. She did this willfully and intentionally to complete the penalty. My daughter understood that the curse had better stop then, or it would carry through to other people.

What would have happened if she had not stopped the curse? What would have happened if I had made excuses or lied and had allowed deception to enter? Suppose that I had called and had the ticket "fixed." Do you know what would have happened? I would have permitted a curse to come into the ministry and, through it, into the people in the church.

Scripture says to pray for all those in authority (1 Timothy 2:1-3). This applies to the husband and father in the home. He permits curses to come in, if he does not resist wrongdoing correctly. It's the same with wives and mothers. What about brothers and sisters? What about grandparents? What about teachers and principals of schools? Those who first permit curses into their own lives, convey curses to others.

All Authority Belongs To Jesus

And Jesus came and spake unto them, saying, *All power is given unto me in heaven and in earth.*

Matthew 28:18

In the book of Revelation, we read John's account of Jesus:

And when I saw him, I fell at his feet as dead. And he laid his right hand upon me, saying unto me, Fear not; I am the first and the last:

I am he that liveth, and was dead; and, behold, I am alive for evermore, Amen; and *have the keys of hell and of death.*

Revelation 1:17-18

All authority belongs to Jesus. He holds the keys of Hell and death. Let's read what Jesus said to Peter about His authority in the book of Matthew:

And Jesus answered and said unto him, Blessed art thou, Simon Bar-jona: for flesh and blood hath not revealed it unto thee, but my Father which is in heaven.

And I say also unto thee, That thou art Peter, and upon this rock I will build my church; and the gates of hell shall not prevail against it.

> *And I will give unto thee the keys of the kingdom of heaven:* and whatsoever thou shalt bind on earth shall be bound in heaven: and whatsoever thou shalt loose on earth shall be loosed in heaven.
>
> Matthew 16:17-19

Here, Jesus gave His authority to Peter. You must understand what God's Word says about your authority and responsibility. You must know this so you do not permit, through ignorance, destructive curses in your life. Jesus gave to you the authority to *cause* the enemy to stop. You are responsible to bind his illegal activities. Do not *permit* him to continue.

You have the spiritual responsibility to stop the enemy's infiltration in your home. You may ask me, "Why didn't you stop your daughter from speeding?" I don't have rule over the *will* of an individual, but only in the *atmosphere* of that individual. I cannot make her decisions. I only can create a spiritual environment of security and protection for her. The decision is ultimately her own.

Understand that when someone delegates to you the authority to act in his behalf, you have his same authority to act. Jesus is the authorized One, the risen One from the dead, and the Keeper of the keys of Hell and death. He delegated this authority to you to remove curses! You, therefore, are responsible to act. If you do not, you permit the enemy to operate. You either permit or cause circumstances to happen.

Use Your Delegated Authority To Reign

Reign Over Sin And Death

Let's consider sin. Jesus conquered sin when He substituted Himself for you on the cross. In Romans, Paul wrote:

> Likewise reckon ye also yourselves to be dead indeed unto sin, but alive unto God through Jesus Christ our Lord.

> *Let* not sin therefore reign in your mortal body, that
> ye should obey it in the lusts thereof.
>
> Romans 6:11-12

Do you *cause* sin to reign? No, you *permit* sin to reign. You see, if sin reigns in your life, you have yielded without resistance to it. If you do not *let* it in, then sin cannot rule you. People who say, "I couldn't help myself. It just happened," escape their responsibility and deceive themselves. Sin cannot enter your life unless you permit it. Sin will rule you, only if you let it. You are directly responsible for the sin that occurs in your body. No one is responsible for another's sin. I am not responsible for your sin, and neither are you responsible for mine. However, my sin does affect your life, and your sin affects my life.

If you give sin the advantage, it will curse you every day of your life in your mind, motivations, and relationships. It will bind and strap you to the ground. Then, you will cry out, "God, there is nothing I can do about it. Sin just has a hold on me." No! It doesn't have a hold on you. You permitted it by yielding to it; you let it hold you captive. Paul continued in Romans 6:

> Neither *yield* ye your members as instruments of
> unrighteousness unto sin: but *yield* yourselves unto God,
> as those that are alive from the dead, and your members
> as instruments of righteousness unto God.
>
> For sin shall not have dominion over you: for ye are
> not under the law, but under *grace.*
>
> Romans 6:13-14

You cannot *make* grace work. You cannot make it flow through you. You *permit* grace to work; or you *permit* sin to work.

You might ask, "How do you let blessings work in your life?" That's easy. Understand that it's your responsibility to permit God to bless you. You see, *you already are blessed:*

> ...with every spiritual blessing in the heavenly places
> in Christ,

> that in the ages to come He might show the exceeding
> riches of His grace in His kindness toward us in Christ Jesus.
>
> Ephesians 1:3; 2:7 (NKJV)

God has lavished and poured out blessings into your life. You don't need to pray, "Lord, bless me." He *already* is blessing you. You simply must *let* Him do it. Does this mean *cause* or *permit*? You cannot *cause* God to do anything; you *permit* Him to work in your life.

In the same way, you *permit* sin; you cannot *cause* sin. That is why Paul wrote in Romans:

> Now then it is no more I that do it, but sin that dwelleth in me.
>
> For I know that in me (that is, in my flesh,) dwelleth no good thing: for to will is present with me; but how to perform that which is good I find not.
>
> For the good that I would I do not: but the evil which I would not, that I do.
>
> Now if I do that I would not, it is no more I that do it, but sin that dwelleth in me.
>
> Romans 7:17-20

Your will doesn't *cause* sin to stop. *You can't will yourself to stop sinning. Sin's power is in your permission. Let* is an awesome word of power. You can let *sin* reign over you by permitting or allowing it into your life. Or you can let *God's grace* reign, which gives *you* the power to reign over sin.

Reign Over Discouragement

Now, let's consider the area of discouragement. Do you realize that you permit all discouragement to happen in your life, and no one else is to blame for your misery? Hebrews says:

> Wherefore seeing we also are compassed about with so great a cloud of witnesses, *let* us lay aside every

weight, and the sin which doth so easily beset us, and *let* us run with patience the race that is set before us,

Looking unto Jesus the author and finisher of our faith; who for the joy that was set before him endured the cross, despising the shame, and is set down at the right hand of the throne of God.

For consider him that endured such contradiction of sinners against himself, lest ye be wearied and faint in your minds.

Hebrews 12:1-3

This Scripture deals with *cause,* not *permission.* To lay aside the discouragements of life, you must *cause* them to move out of the way. Otherwise, the curse of discouragement will have you. If you sit idle even for one day, you will become discouraged. If you sit alone on your day off and do nothing, watch what will happen. As you look at your life, Satan will paint a picture of destruction. You'll look at your past; he will tell you how miserable you are. Then, he will convince you that you are going nowhere.

Unless you take a causative action, you will never rid yourself of discouragement. You must take the advantage. As we just read, you need to look unto Jesus, the author and finisher of your faith. Engage in the race that is set before you. If you don't move, discouragement will have you by default. Then, you probably will blame others for your misery, when the responsibility is really yours. No one is responsible for allowing your misery except you.

Reign Over Strife

What about strife? Paul wrote:

Let nothing be done through *strife* or vainglory; but in lowliness of mind *let* each esteem other better than themselves.

Philippians 2:3

As we studied earlier, the word *strife* means "to be at odds with." You *permit* strife to happen. It does not occur without an advantage. Strife is a curse, a proclamation of ill will, and a detriment. It zaps your strength and motivation. You become argumentative, and find yourself affected by life's negativity, because you have *let* strife in.

It might surprise you that I choose not to talk to some people. I do not listen to strife or permit it to be around me. Otherwise, it would become a part of me. Then, I would preach bitter messages and convey strife to the people in my church. You see, my freedom from strife produces their freedom; but my bondage also can produce their bondage to curses, and I simply cannot afford that.

You must replace strife with peace. Jesus said:

> Peace I leave with you, my peace I give unto you: not as the world giveth, give I unto you. *Let* not your heart be troubled, neither *let* it be afraid.
>
> John 14:27

Paul wrote this about peace:

> And *let* the peace of God rule in your hearts, to the which also ye are called in one body; and be ye thankful.
> *Let* the word of Christ dwell in you richly in all wisdom; teaching and admonishing one another in psalms and hymns and spiritual songs, singing with grace in your hearts to the Lord.
>
> Colossians 3:15-16

Do you *cause* the peace of God to rule? No! You cannot *make* peace happen. You *permit* the peace of God to reign in your life. If you want peace to rule, you must give permission, or yield, to the Holy Spirit, Who is peace. Quiet yourself and permit God's peace to reign in you.

Do you *cause* the Word of God to dwell in your heart richly, or do you *permit* it? How do you get the Word to reign in your heart? You cannot sit back and say, "Okay, Word of God, just rule my life. I give You permission." No! You must *cause* God's Word to rule your life. You must act. Sow that Word into your own life. Go to where you can hear or read the Word of God. If you don't act first to create an advantage for yourself, the enemy will have the advantage because of your ignorance.

Reign With Strong Confession

Keep your words in line with the Word of God. Hold fast to your profession. Otherwise Satan will use negative words to restrict God's Word from having an effect in your life. These negative words can come even from your own mouth. Sometimes, when we pray liberating prayers, we are really praying to free ourselves from our own words.

> Seeing then that we have a great high priest, that is passed into the heavens, Jesus the Son of God, *let* us hold fast our profession.
> For we have not an high priest which cannot be touched with the feeling of our infirmities; but was in all points tempted like as we are, yet without sin.
> *Let* us therefore come boldly unto the throne of grace, that we may obtain mercy, and find grace to help in time of need.
> Hebrews 4:14-16

The word *let* in these verses is the word *cause*. When you profess the Word of God, you cause your words to be stable.

How do you go to the throne of grace? Do you say, "Well, God, if You want to bless me, bring me into Your throne room. I'm ready, just do it"? That would be *permission*. No, you must *cause* yourself to come into the throne room of grace. How do you enter?

Having therefore, brethren, boldness to enter into

94

the holiest *by the blood of Jesus,*
By a new and living way, which he hath consecrated
for us, *through the veil, that is to say, his flesh.*

Hebrews 10:19-20

You take the truth about the Blood of Jesus, and cause
yourself to believe it. Refusing to hear the voice of accusation,
ridicule, and negativity, you cause yourself to come into the
throne of God through the Blood of Jesus and the veil of His
flesh. Verses 21-22 continue:

And having an high priest over the house of God;
Let us draw near with a true heart in full assurance of
faith, having our hearts sprinkled from an evil conscience,
and our bodies washed with pure water.

Hebrews 10:21-22

Who is to take the action here? Are we to *permit* the drawing
near, or are we to *cause* the drawing near? If you want to be close
to God, you must *cause* yourself to get close to Him.
Verses 23-24 read:

Let us hold fast the profession of our faith without
wavering; (for he is faithful that promised;)
And *let* us consider one another to provoke unto love
and to good works.

Hebrews 10:23-24

How do you hold fast your profession? Do you *permit* or
cause your words of faith to come forth? Obviously, you *cause*
your words.

How do you provoke others to good works? People have
said to me, "Pastor Gary, you are always urging me to move,
and I'm tired. I just want to be in a place where I'm not
provoked."

I have told them, "Then you will be in a place that will make you comfortable; and in doing so, you ignorantly will permit curse. Knowing the Word of God will provoke you and have an impact on your life. I am not an effective pastor if I don't provoke you to good works, trying to cause you to act." Some people would prefer to be where they don't know the truth, so they can avoid confrontation and a provocation to action.

Some may regard this book as "a heavy teaching," because it puts biblical responsibility upon them and provokes them to good works. *Identify And Remove Curses* reveals how people can either permit or stop curses, and permit or stop blessings.

You see, if you *cause* yourself to submit to God, to obey His Word, and to live under the Blood of Jesus, then you yield to "every good and every perfect gift...from above..." (James 1:17). You give the Holy Spirit *permission* to rule in your home, as a consequence of your actions of obedience. This is blessing.

If, however, on the other hand, you *cause* yourself not to live according to God's purposes for your life, then you yield yourself to the devil. By default, you give him *permission* to do every evil work in your life and in the lives of those around you. This is the consequence of your actions of disobedience. This is curse.

Today, I encourage you—like Moses urged the Children of Israel—to choose blessing, not curse. Do this not only for your sake, but for your children and their children:

> I call heaven and earth to record this day against you, that *I have set before you life and death, blessing and cursing: therefore choose life, that both thou and thy seed may live.*
> Deuteronomy 30:19

How To Cause And Permit Good Circumstances

You must understand biblically what you cause and permit. *What you let is what you get.* What you don't know definitely will hurt you, because unknowingly you can *let* bad circumstances into your life. So, how do you *let* in the good?

Confess The Word

First, you confess what the Word of God says that you are and what you have. You sow to yourself and stand on that Word, so it will become an advantage. You must hold fast your profession. Out of your own mouth come blessing or cursing. So, if you want to create blessing, you must speak forth the Word of God.

Take Defensive Action

Next, you must act against the enemy that is challenging your authority. If you do not resist, you will permit that challenge. You must rise up against the enemy's efforts against you. Remember:

> Submit yourselves therefore to God. Resist the devil, and he will flee from you.
>
> James 4:7

Take Offensive, Obedient Action

Then, you must act—to cause the result you want—by doing the Word of God. So, you speak what God's Word says. You actively resist the enemy's curse that he is trying to assign to you. Then, you willfully do what the Word of God says, and *cause* that Word to have an effect in your life. Do it.

"But what if it looks like everything around me is going to fail?" Do it.

"Well, what if it doesn't look like anything is going to happen?" Do it. Why? Because if you don't do it, you are self-deceived and self-cursed. If you don't, you *permit* the curse to come. A man who does not do the Word of God is self-cursed in every level and circumstance of life.

Stop the enemy in Jesus' Name. Cause the action. Speak the words. Resist the curse that is trying to alight upon you. Turn it around by *causing* an action that will bring positive results. What action can you take to invoke blessing? What can you *cause* to happen? Remember, *to let* means "to cause" or "to permit."

97

You *let* events happen in your life. Unless you *let* Him, God cannot do what He wants to do. Why? It is because you have *permitted* other circumstances to rule and influence your life.

Knowledge of and obedience to the Word of God is the key. So, first apply yourself to knowledge; then do it.

> Buy the truth, and sell it not; also wisdom, and instruction, and understanding.
>
> Proverbs 23:23

Let these become the most desirable entities in your life. Let your knowledge of and experience with God be the most valuable possessions you will ever have. Come out of curse, and let God bless you. Remember, "the curse causeless [without advantage] shall not come"!!

Learn to forgive and forebear. Believe the best in everyone, while allowing your spirit to be sensitive and aware of anything pointing to the contrary. Realize that as *you* change, you release the penetrating power of God's grace to others around you. Don't pre-judge anyone or anything before you know the truth; and even then, let your words be positive, not negative. Let's close this chapter with this powerful prayer:

> Father, I thank You that by the power of the Blood of Jesus You have forgiven and liberated me. No longer must I live with hurts and the forces of curses and negative words—both those I have spoken and those that others have spoken against me. I release Your anointing on all those I have spoken against, and I cast down the accuser of the brethren in Jesus' Name.
>
> I raise the shield of faith as a standard to quench the fiery darts of the enemy. With the sword of Your living Word, I cut through all curses in my life. I command the power of negative words of curse spoken against me to be bound and nullified. I command these evil words to return to the sender. I decree that all demonic spirits

have no advantage over me, and every snare set to entrap me is broken. Father, You have redeemed me for Your purpose. I now set my course according to Your will, King of Glory.

Father, thank You for the anointing and power that is on Your Word to liberate me. You have destined me by Your Holy Spirit to remove all the curses of the enemy. You have given me revelation knowledge. I have the mind of Christ. I will not permit the curse of sin to have rule and influence in my life. I reckon myself dead to sin and alive unto God.

Father, the Blood of Jesus has washed me. I believe that when You raised Jesus from the dead, You forgave all my sins. Jesus, I receive You into my heart. I confess that You are the Lord of my life. I am dead, and my life is hidden with Christ in God. I do not permit sin to reign in this temple. I am destined to let Your grace and Your blessing rule, Lord; and I permit You to reign in my life. I submit myself to you, resist the devil, and he must flee.

Ignorance will not rule my life. I take authority over every curse, proclamation of harm, word of destruction, discouragement, and all strife, by the power of the Name of Jesus. I cast down accusation. The curse causeless shall not come upon me. I cause the love of God to rush out of my heart, and I look for every opportunity to release the Word of God. Lord, Your blessing of peace reigns in my mind, now. In Jesus' Name. Amen.

6
Lift Financial Curses

Now, you have come to the last—but very important—chapter in this book, *Identify And Remove Curses*. In this section, we will study one of the most significant areas of affliction in the Church today.

Every week, my staff and I pray over multitudes of prayer requests that come into the Gary Whetstone Worldwide Ministries. We also have seen tens of thousands of people in prayer lines around the world. During this contact with the Body of Christ, I have discovered that the greatest challenge facing a very large percentage of Christians is finances. Their finances are not increasing, and they cannot pay all their bills. Mounting debt keeps them in a vicious cycle of borrowing. The Bible calls this simply a curse.

As you begin to read this chapter, open your heart wide to the work of the Holy Spirit. It is time to lift the curse off you and your family's lives. It is time to break the financial hindrances off the vision that God has for you. Now, let's look at the Bible to see how to destroy financial curses in your life.

God Cares About Your Finances

The Word of God has more to say about finances, property, stewardship, and the use of material things than any other subject! This topic is very significant to God. *Your* financial condition matters to Him—even more than it does to you.

Give with a Pure Heart

Let's look at the story of a couple in the Bible: Ananias and

Sapphira. You can read the full account in Acts 4:32-5:16. This husband and wife were aspiring to leadership in their New Testament congregation. In this church, believers were selling their land and properties, then giving the proceeds of the sales to the church. The congregation lived in harmony and no one lacked anything. They regularly experienced God's awesome power.

Now, when Ananias and Sapphira sold a piece of their property, together they agreed to withhold a portion from God. Then, the couple lied by understating the sales price of the land. As a tragic result, they dropped dead instantly.

You might ask, "Why would God be upset with Ananias and Sapphira? After all, they freely and sacrificially gave after they had sold their land." Yes, this couple gave a large, sacrificial offering, but they sinned in the process. Ananias and Sapphira lied to the Holy Ghost.

> But Peter said, Ananias, why hath Satan filled thine heart to *lie to the Holy Ghost,* and to keep back part of the price of the land?
> Whiles it remained, was it not thine own? and after it was sold, was it not in thine own power? why hast thou conceived this thing in thine heart? *thou hast not lied unto men, but unto God.*
>
> Acts 5:3-4

Remember, God sees past your actions to your true attitudes and the motivations of your heart.

> The Lord seeth not as man seeth; for man looketh on the outward appearance, but the Lord looketh on the heart.
>
> 1 Samuel 16:7b

Although the outward appearance was that of a significantly large gift, the hearts of Ananias and Sapphira were wicked. The

Amplified version clarifies this:

> But Peter said, Ananias, why has Satan filled your heart that you should lie to and attempt to deceive the Holy Spirit, and should [in violation of your promise] withdraw secretly and appropriate to your own use part of the price from the sale of the land?
>
> As long as it remained unsold, was it not still your own? And [even] after it was sold, was not [the money] at your disposal and under your control? Why then, is it that you have proposed and purposed in your heart to do this thing?—How could you have the heart to do such a deed? You have not (simply) lied to men—playing false and showing yourself utterly deceitful—but to God.
>
> Acts 5:3-4 (AMP)

If your motivations for giving are sinful, it does not matter how big your gift is or how much you sacrificed to give it. Sin is a stench to God. So, if you want to show your love to and please God, keep your heart pure in everything you do—especially in your giving!

God's Guarantees

How can you be sure that your heart is pure regarding your money? Jesus gave a test for us to see if our motives are right. He said:

> Lay not up for yourselves treasures upon earth, where moth and rust doth corrupt, and where thieves break through and steal:
>
> But lay up for yourselves treasures in heaven, where neither moth nor rust doth corrupt, and where thieves do not break through nor steal:
>
> *For where your treasure is, there will your heart be also.*
> Matthew 6:19-21

What is important to you? Where do you put your money? Do you spend your money on earthly treasures and possessions or in the work of God's Kingdom? Where you put your money will show where your heart is. Do you give to the work of the ministry to see souls saved, healed, baptized, and set free? Or do you hoard your money only to buy boats, clothes, jewelry, cars, and other items?

Let me make this clear. It is not wrong to have nice possessions. In fact, God will bless you when you obey Him. However, He wants your heart to be in the right place. The choice is yours:

- *Selfishly hoard* your possessions, only for them to deteriorate.

- Or, *selflessly release* what you have, and God will guarantee that it will not deteriorate. Not only that, He will multiply it back to you!

Give, and it shall be given unto you; good measure, pressed down, and shaken together, and running over, shall men give into your bosom. For with the same measure that ye mete withal it shall be measured to you again.

Luke 6:38

Yes, God promises to multiply your giving back to you and He will preserve it from destruction. You see, if your treasure is in the earth and in the things of the earth, the Scripture says that it will become corrupt and rusted. Or, moths will eat it. Thieves will steal it. On the other hand, if your treasure is in Heaven and in the work of God, He personally will guarantee that your investment will not become corrupt or rusted. No moths will eat it. Thieves will not get through to steal it.

Why? It is because your treasure—and, therefore, your heart—is in Heaven. Do you see how powerful that is? Your giving shows where your heart is!

Give Sacrificially

Always remember that God does not look at the *outward appearance* of your offerings, but at the *inward condition* of your heart. Likewise, He does not look at the *amount* of your offering, but at your *sacrifice*. In the Gospel of Mark is an excellent example of this:

> And Jesus sat over against the treasury, and beheld how the people cast money into the treasury: and *many that were rich cast in much.*
> And there came *a certain poor widow, and she threw in two mites, which make a farthing [a total of about a penny].*
> And he called unto him his disciples, and saith unto them, Verily I say unto you, *That this poor widow hath cast more in, than all they which have cast into the treasury:*
> For all they did cast in of their abundance; but she of her want [out of her own need] did cast in all that she had, even all her living.
>
> Mark 12:41-44

Here, Jesus said that a tiny gift from a widow meant more to Him than large offerings from the rich! Why? She sacrificially gave out of her need. Her gift was very valuable to her, and so it was to God.

On the other hand, the wealthy gave what was left over. Since they did not sacrifice, their gifts were less valuable to them, and, therefore, meant less to God.

You might say, "Well, God understands what I'm facing. He certainly would not require me to give anything more than from what's left over." My friend, it is quite the contrary.

Do you remember David's sacrifice at Ornan's threshingfloor? We studied this story in the second chapter of this book. Recall that when David made his sacrifice, he insisted that he pay full price to Ornan for the floor, saying:

...I will verily buy it for the full price: for I will not take that which is thine for the Lord, nor offer burnt offerings *without cost.*

1 Chronicles 21:24

David refused to sacrifice (give) to God that which cost him nothing. He understood sacrificial giving. I encourage you not to give to God from what's left over in your life. Instead, give sacrificially. Then, get ready for your breakthrough!

Tithing

Tithing is a very critical part of your giving. You must handle it correctly, or your life will be cursed. Now, let's look at the tithe, or the firstfruits. The word *tithe* means a tenth or ten percent. In the Old Testament, the *firstfruits* were the very first part of the harvest.

The Tithe Belongs To God
The Word of God declares that the firstfruits and the tithe belong to the Lord:

Honour the Lord with thy substance, and with the *firstfruits* of all of thine increase.

Proverbs 3:9

And all the *tithe* of the land, whether of the seed of the land, or of the fruit of the tree, is the Lord's: it is holy unto the Lord.

Leviticus 27:30

You must understand God's view of the tithe. It is very significant to Him. How you handle your giving to the Lord determines whether blessing or cursing occurs in your life. I cannot emphasize this enough.

Whether your revenue comes from the sale of property,

income from labor, or some type of a profit-sharing program, you must give ten percent to God. No matter how your revenue comes, a tenth of the entire gross increase should go into the hands of the Church for God's work.

The Terms Of The Covenant

When you accepted Jesus Christ as your Lord and Savior, you entered into a covenant with God. Now, each time you receive Communion, you celebrate the Lord's death and resurrection. By this, you recognize and reaffirm your covenant with God. Now, you must understand the terms of your covenant with God.

You see, every clearly defined covenant in the Bible has two facets:

- Adherence and obedience to the covenant brings blessing.

- Disobedience and violation of the covenant brings curse.

The only way to obtain deliverance and blessing is through obedience to the terms of your covenantal relationship with God. If, instead, you violate the covenant, you open the door for curses to enter your life. *Blessings and curses happen in your life by your choice, not by chance.* Remember, by your actions or lack of actions, you *choose* blessings or curses. (See Deuteronomy 30:19.)

Tithing Yields Blessings

Most scholars agree that Abraham (then known as Abram) was the first to give tithes to God. Let's examine the circumstances that led to the first tithe recorded in the Bible.

In the midst of a large battle, four kings captured Abraham's nephew Lot plus Lot's family and possessions. To free his relatives and their goods, Abraham fought and won a battle in the Valley of Shaveh with the four enemy kings. After Abraham's victory, he presented a *tenth of all the spoils* from his battle to a priest named Melchizedek. Notice, that Abraham's tithe was not a tenth of the *leftovers*. It was a tenth of *everything* that was then in his hand. Abraham tithed on the entirety of his income—his "gross receipts"!

> And Melchizedek king of Salem brought forth bread and wine: and he was the priest of the most high God.
> And he blessed him, and said, Blessed be Abram of the most high God, possessor of heaven and earth:
> And blessed be the most high God, which hath delivered thine enemies into thy hand. *And he gave him tithes of all.*
>
> Genesis 14:18–20

After this time of giving, one of Abraham's defeated enemies—the King of Sodom—tried to convince Abraham to keep the spoils for himself. However, Abraham refused, replying that only God—not the King of Sodom—could take credit for the blessing on Abraham's life.

> But Abram said to the king of Sodom, I have lifted up my hand and sworn to the Lord, God Most High, the possessor and maker of heaven and earth,
> That I would not take a thread or a shoelace or anything that is yours, lest you should say, I have made Abram rich.
>
> Genesis 14:22-23 (AMP)

As a result Abraham became the wealthiest man in the world, and God received the glory. Remember, God had decreed:

> And I will make of thee [Abram] a great nation, and I will bless thee, and make thy name great; and thou shalt be a blessing.
>
> Genesis 12:2

Lie: "Tithing Does Not Apply
To New Testament Christians"

Many have argued, saying, "Well, that is the Old Testament. That's under the Law—the old covenant. We no longer have to fulfill any of those old, scriptural understandings. We're under the new covenant of the New Testament. God knows our needs and situations today. We don't have to tithe."

Remember, Abraham began tithing *before* Moses gave the Law. Nevertheless, God *does* know exactly where you are, today. That is why you can "come boldly unto the throne of grace" to "obtain mercy, and find grace to help in time of need" (Hebrews 4:16). However, giving to God the firstfruits and the tithe of all that He entrusts you with is not an option. *He requires obedience.* You cannot plead or reason your way out of it. You simply must obey. This is how blessings come into your life.

Let me explain how tithing carries over from the old to the new covenant, and why we must tithe still today. After Abraham first tithed, it became a law in the Old Testament. The people's tithes supported the Levitical priesthood and supplied all their daily needs at the temple. Now, let's look together in the last book of the old covenant:

> For I am the Lord, I change not; therefore ye sons of Jacob are not consumed.
> Even from the days of your fathers ye are gone away from mine ordinances, and have not kept them. Return unto me, and I will return to you, saith the Lord of hosts. But ye said, Wherein shall we return?
> Malachi 3:6-7

The next statement is very powerful. Notice God's first sentence, here:

> *Will a man rob God?* Yet ye have robbed me. But ye say, Wherein [God,] have we robbed thee? [God replied:] In tithes and offerings.

You are cursed with a curse: for ye have robbed me,
even this *whole nation.*

Malachi 3:8-9

Notice the first word in the above passage. Here, the Word
of God does not say "can." It says simply "will." This means that
the person has a choice. If he chooses to rob God, certain
detrimental consequences—a curse—will come. On the other
hand, if he chooses not to rob God, then blessings will come.

Here lies the greatest key to causing financial challenges in
your life. By robbing God "in tithes and offerings," you open the
door to bring curse not only upon yourself, but also upon your
family, the church you attend, your work place, and ultimately
all your relationships!

So, what does the Bible say? Does it say, "You are cursed,
and there is nothing you can do?" No, the Word says:

Bring ye all the tithes into the storehouse, that there
may be *meat* in mine house.

Malachi 3:10a

In John 4 verses 34 to 38, Jesus amplified what that *meat* is.
He said:

...My *meat* is to do the will of him that sent me, and to
finish his work.

John 4:34

So, we are to bring the tithe into "the storehouse," which is
the local church that does the will of God. This is the place that
feeds the Word of God to men, women, and children. For you,
in particular, "the storehouse" is where you are receiving the
strengthening Word of God. The Bible continues in Malachi:

And prove me now herewith, saith the Lord of hosts, if
I will not open you the windows of heaven, and pour you

110

out a blessing, that there shall not be room enough to receive it.

Malachi 3:10b

In other words, God is saying to you, "Look, now I am about to bring blessing when you give your tithe." The next verses say:

And I will rebuke the devourer for your sakes, and he shall not destroy the fruits of your ground; neither shall your vine cast her fruit before the time in the field, saith the Lord of hosts.
And *all nations* shall call you blessed.

Malachi 3:11-12a

Why will you be blessed? It is because you have a covenant with God and you honor (bless) God with the tithe, or the firstfruits. Verse 12 continues:

For ye shall be a delightsome land, saith the Lord....

Malachi 3:12b

"That's wonderful," you might say, "but this is still the Old Testament. Where is tithing in the New Testament?" I am glad you asked! It does tie together. You see, the Bible is a continuum. By knowing the Old Testament, you can better understand the New Testament. Remember, it is important that you understand the Word of God as a whole—not merely in parts.

In the previous pages, I have laid a foundation from the Old Testament that we can build upon, now. Remember, Jesus came not to throw away the Old Testament, but to fulfill it. He said:

Think not that I am come to destroy the law, or the prophets: I am not come to destroy, but to fulfill [the law].

Matthew 5:17

With our study of tithing in the Old Testament firmly in your mind, let's look at the book of Hebrews. Remember, this is in the New Testament.

> For this Melchizedek, king of Salem, priest of the Most High God, who met Abraham returning from the slaughter of the kings and blessed him,
> to whom also Abraham gave a tenth part of all...
> *but [Melchizedek was] made like the Son of God [Jesus], remains a priest continually.*
> Hebrews 7:1-3 (NKJV)

Then, verse seven contains a tremendous revelation about giving your tithe:

> Now beyond all contradiction the lesser is blessed by the better.
> Here mortal men receive tithes, but *there he receives them, of whom it is witnessed that he lives.*
> Hebrews 7:7-8 (NKJV)

Here, the Bible blasts away some of the false teaching and thoughts that have kept the Body of Christ cursed. This passage explains that today—in the covenant of the New Testament—there are *two* who receive your tithes. One is the ministry where you place the tenth of your gross revenue. There, your tithe goes into the hands of a person. Now, this is a mortal person, who will die one day (unless Jesus returns first). The second One Who receives your tithe is the One "of whom it is witnessed that he lives." If you continue to read Hebrews, it becomes clear that this is Jesus. *In Heaven, Jesus Himself receives your tithes!*

> And it is yet far more evident if, in the likeness of Melchizedek, there arises another priest
> who has come, not according to the law of a fleshly commandment, but according to the power of an endless

life.

For He testifies: "You are a priest forever According to the order of Melchizedek." [This is quoted from Psalm 110:4, illustrating that Jesus fulfilled this prophecy.]

by so much more Jesus has become a surety [guarantee] of a better covenant.

And there were many priests, because they were prevented by death from continuing.

But He, because He continues forever, has an unchangeable priesthood.

Hebrews 7:15-17, 22-24 (NKJV)

Did you know that Jesus actually receives your tithes in Heaven, today? Yes, He does, because the tithe is *holy to God*. It is His. However, He trusts you with it for a time to see if you will be a robber.

What Are The Results Of Robbing God?

Remember the Scripture in Malachi 3:8 that asks, "Will a man rob God?" What is robbery? To understand it better, let's compare robbery with other forms of stealing.

- *Embezzlement* is skimming away money illegally by submitting false receipts or another similar way.

- *Theft* is the act of sneaking into a place and simply stealing the possession of another.

- *Robbery*, however, is the only kind of theft that implies the potential of bodily harm.

For example, think of the term *armed robbery*. This is the act of stealing a person's property while using a weapon of violence (such as a gun) to hurt him or another. You see, robbery is not stealing something simply for one's own desire, betterment, or gain. No, robbery also creates bodily harm.

You might ask, "What 'bodily harm' exists when I don't give my tithe to God?" The body that you harm is the Body of Christ! You see, when you withhold the tithe from God, this prevents men, women, and children from hearing the Gospel of Jesus Christ. Your lack of tithing, inhibits the Body of Christ from feeding, strengthening, and nourishing itself. The Body of Christ cannot reach the world as effectively to minister to the lost and dying generation—one that Jesus paid for with His Blood.

In this form of robbery, you not only hurt God and the Body of Christ, but you also deprive yourself and your family of blessings. However, according to Malachi, when you give your tithes and offerings to God, He opens the windows of Heaven and rebukes the devourer. He blesses everything around you.

Remember, this is not about what man thinks is fair. This is about a just God Who has given His only begotten Son for you. All He asks from you is that you honor Him by giving to Him the tenth. Let God bless you. Give to Him your tithes and offerings.

Reverse Financial Curse
To Receive Financial Blessing

The psalmist declared:

> Let them shout for joy, and be glad, that favour my righteous cause: yea, let them say continually, Let the Lord be magnified, which hath pleasure in the prosperity of his servant.
>
> Psalm 35:27

I shared earlier in Leviticus 27, verse 30, the Bible declares that the tithe "is holy unto the Lord":

> And all the tithe of the land, whether of the seed of the land, or of the fruit of the tree, is the Lord's: it is holy unto the Lord.
>
> Leviticus 27:30

Now, picture your life. God entrusts you with 100 percent. One-tenth is His own—set apart to God, hallowed for His use, and only designed for God. *It is His.* You have the greatest opportunity to bring blessing and to reverse the curse through *one simple act.* How? Look at everything that comes into your life—your gross revenue. Then, calculate ten percent of that figure, and give it to God. Do this regularly and without fail.

As you write your tithe check, give cash, or use a debit or bank card, lift it before the living Lord, Jesus Christ. According to the seventh chapter of Hebrews and the third chapter of Malachi, pray this aloud as you tithe:

Lord Jesus, receive this tithe. I bless and honor You with the firstfruits of all my increase, now. Please forgive me for not tithing to You in the past.

Father, forgive me for robbing You, the Body of Christ, myself, and those around me. Almighty God, today, I present my tithe to You. Now, prove Yourself, according to Your Word. I believe that You are the covenant-keeping God Who breaks the power of curse; opens the windows of Heaven; and invokes blessings upon my life, family, church, community, and work. Now, I am blessed coming in and going out.

In Jesus' Name, I command the curse of debt over my life to stop, now! I break the curse of premature delivery of dreams and visions in my life. I declare that God's dreams and visions for my life will come in His proper timing. In Jesus' Name, I stop the power of the devourer this day in my life.

From this day forth, I shall tithe continually. Therefore, I will live under an open Heaven with a perpetual rain of the Lord's blessings from on high. In Jesus' Name. Amen.

Hallelujah! If you just prayed this aloud and made a commitment to the Lord to tithe from now on, no man or demon can reverse the blessings that God has in store for you! Remember, *you* are in charge of your destiny in relationship to this covenant, because *you choose to obey or disobey the terms of the covenant.* God always upholds His side. The rest is up to you. It's that simple.

Your tithe should go to your local church. Today, however, if you do not have a local church that you consistently attend, I encourage you to begin to tithe to this ministry: Gary Whetstone Worldwide Ministries (G.W.W.M.) at P.O. Box 10050 in Wilmington, DE 19850 U.S.A. This global ministry is good, hot soil to sow your tithe into. Then, when you find the local church that feeds you, pay your tithe there, and continue your seed to G.W.W.M. as your missions offering.

Don't forget, Satan can get the advantage over you in only one way. That is if you give it to him. Remember the Scripture that has become the theme of this entire book:

As the bird by wandering, as the swallow by flying, so the curse causeless shall not come.

Proverbs 26:2

We have studied extensively the word *causeless* which means "without advantage." Do not open the door for the enemy to have the advantage over you by your speech, thoughts, beliefs, actions, and, finally, *how you give.*

Be blessed! Let God's Word burn strongly in you. Don't let it be "head knowledge" only. Get this revelation into your spirit. Read this book again and again. Share with your friends and family this awesome book. Act on it. Speak the Word of God. Anchor the truth in your life. Release from your hand the tithe—that which also will bless you. Give it to God. Right now, reverse the curse! It is your right to be free!

A Word From The Lord

As I write this now, I sense the power of the Holy Spirit

rising up within my spirit. He has a special Word to help you right where you are, today. Hear this with your spiritual ears:

"For this day," saith the Spirit of the Lord, "shall be a cleansing of the clouds of obscurity from before your eyes. That which had become darkened unto you—obscuring your path, restricting your future, and limiting that which I am doing—shall from this day forward be seen no more.

"The enemy has come before you—day after day, and year after year. He has stood as a mockery of the very God to Whom you belong, for Whom you have been sent to represent, and Who lives through you. From this day, shall you step on an even place where the enemy is your footstool. For this is not a day for you to negotiate with your opponent. This is the day for you to crush the serpent's head, to take the power of curse and render it powerless.

"Rise up, *knowing that you know* that in Him all things which pertain to life and godliness have been given unto you. Be the person of blessing that God has sent you into the earth to be. Fulfill that destiny only designed by God for you. For in so doing, you shall liberate not only yourself, your family, and your city, but you shall be a liberator in this world. It shall be known of you that you have become one that repairs the breech and restores the streets to dwell in.

"Be not shocked," saith the Spirit of God, "when the power of conviction is so strong upon your life that none can withstand the very wisdom of the Spirit of God Whom speaks through you. Be not shocked when sin becomes utterly sinful before you, and the heart cry of righteousness is established in you. It shall rise as a standard from which you will not compromise. Neither will you allow the gainsaying voice of those who know not Me to bring within your way a compromised lifestyle.

"This day, come ye apart, and be separate," saith the Spirit of the Lord. "I am there to bless you."

Praise God! What an ending that is to a book! This is the time, my friend. Break the chains. Let that prophetic Word from the Holy Spirit burn inside you. It's *your* time to reign and prevail. Live blessed, and let nothing bring curse into your life ever again!

Appendix

How To Receive God's Free Gift

Have you ever received God's free gift of Eternal Life? Do you know for certain that if you were to die today you would go to Heaven? Everlasting life is a gift from God. When Jesus Christ died on the cross and rose bodily from the grave, He paid for our sins. The Bible says:

> For God so loved the world, that he gave his only begotten Son, that whosoever believeth in him should not perish, but have everlasting life.
>
> John 3:16

Since Jesus paid for this gift, we don't have to. We only need to receive it.

> But as many as received him, to them gave he power to become the sons of God, even to them that believe on his name.
>
> John 1:12

> For by grace are ye saved through faith; and that not of yourselves: it is the gift of God:
> Not of works, lest any man should boast.
>
> Ephesians 2:8-9

The way to receive God's gift simply is to believe God's Word and receive it by the profession of your mouth.

That if you confess with your mouth, "Jesus is Lord," and believe in your heart that God raised him from the dead, you will be saved.
...It is with your heart that you believe and are justified, and it is with your mouth that you confess and are saved.
Romans 10:9-10 (NIV)

Now, pray this prayer aloud:

Father, thank You for loving me. Thank You for giving Your Son, Jesus, to die for me.
Jesus Christ, Son of God, come into my heart, forgive me of my sins, and be my Lord and Savior. Jesus, I declare that You are Lord, and that You are Lord of my life. In Jesus' Name. Amen.

You are now born again!
All believers are entitled to over 7,000 promises that God has written in His Word. That now includes you! To learn about these promises, attend church regularly. If you are in the area of New Castle, Delaware, please join us for services at Victory Christian Fellowship. Visit our web site at www.gwwm.com for directions and more information. I encourage you to attend a local church that teaches the uncompromised Word of God—the Bible. Daily spend time in prayer, fellowship with the Lord, and reading the Bible. This will help you to understand the "new creature" that you have become now in Christ.

...If any man be in Christ, he is a *new creature:* old things are passed away; behold, all things are become new.
2 Corinthians 5:17

For more information about your new life in Christ, please order *The Victorious Walk* book. *Purchase this book wherever fine Christian products are sold in your area. Or, see the product list and order form at the back of this book.*

Have You Received The Holy Spirit Since You Believed?

In Acts 19:2 (NKJV), the apostle Paul asked the Ephesians this very important question:

"Did you receive the Holy Spirit when you believed?"

The question startled them, and they answered:

"We have not so much as heard whether there is a Holy Spirit."

Later, when they prayed together:

...The Holy Spirit came upon them, and they spoke with tongues and prophesied.

Acts 19:6

What Is The Baptism In The Holy Spirit?

The Baptism in the Holy Spirit is an anointing of power, an enabling or ability from God in the believer's life which equips him or her to witness fully of the life of Jesus Christ.

The Holy Spirit was given on the Day of Pentecost and has never left. This is a distinct experience from conversion to Christ. The Baptism in the Holy Spirit was a separate experience in Jesus' life when He was water baptized, in the apostles' lives on the Day of Pentecost, and in the believer's life today.

Who Is It For, And What Is It?

The Baptism in the Holy Spirit is for believers, because the world cannot receive Him. This experience is to equip and empower believers to worship God supernaturally. The first move of the Holy Spirit when He came upon the early Christians was to speak the praises of God through them (Acts 2:11).

This Baptism is God's outpouring of His Spirit into a person's life to equip him or her to be a witness of Jesus. Christ said:

> But ye shall receive power, after that the Holy Ghost is come upon you: and ye shall be witnesses unto me both in Jerusalem, and in all Judaea, and in Samaria, and unto the uttermost part of the earth.
>
> Acts 1:8

Why Be Baptized In The Holy Spirit?

It is God's will for every believer to be baptized in the Holy Spirit. It is His desire that you overflow with His Spirit continually. Jesus COMMANDED the disciples not to leave Jerusalem until they had been endued with power.

> And, behold, I send the promise of my Father upon you: but tarry ye in the city of Jerusalem, until ye be endued with power from on high.
>
> Luke 24:49

In Ephesians 5:17-18, the Word of God says that believers are to understand (comprehend, grasp, perceive) what the will of the Lord is. Also, they are to be filled with the Holy Spirit.

> Wherefore be ye not unwise, but understanding what the will of the Lord is.

> And be not drunk with wine, wherein is excess; but be filled with the Spirit.
>
> Ephesians 5:17-18

Jesus also said those who believe on Him SHOULD receive the Holy Spirit:

> (But this spake he of the Spirit, which they that believe on him should receive: for the Holy Ghost was not yet given; because that Jesus was not yet glorified.)
>
> John 7:39

How Do I Receive The Baptism In The Holy Spirit?

Ask and you will receive. Knowing that it is God's will for us to be filled with the Holy Spirit gives us confidence in asking Him to baptize us in the Holy Spirit.

> And this is the confidence that we have in him, that, if we ask any thing according to his will, he heareth us: ...If we know that he hear us, whatsoever we ask, we know that we have the petitions that we desired of him.
>
> 1 John 5:14-15

> ...Ask, and it shall be given you;
> how much more shall your heavenly Father give the Holy Spirit to them that ask him?
>
> Luke 11:9a, 13b

What Happens When I Receive This Baptism?

New Language

One of the first experiences that we have when we are filled with the Holy Spirit is that God gives to us a supernatural language. Our hearts are turned more completely to God, to whom we were reconciled already in Jesus Christ when we were born again. Jesus said:

> And these signs shall follow them that believe...they shall speak with new tongues.
>
> Mark 16:17

The Gentiles in the house of Cornelius spoke with tongues when the Holy Spirit came on them (Acts 10:44-48). Likewise, as we studied earlier, the people of Ephesus spoke in tongues when the Holy Spirit came upon them:

> And when Paul had laid hands on them, the Holy Spirit came upon them, and they spoke with tongues and prophesied.
>
> Acts 19:6 (NKJV)

What Does Speaking In Tongues Do?

Praises The Lord In A God-Appointed Way

> ...When thou shalt bless with the spirit...
> ...thou verily givest thanks well....
>
> 1 Corinthians 14:16-17

Edifies Spiritually

> He that speaketh in an unknown tongue edifieth himself.
>
> 1 Corinthians 14:4a

Reminds Of The Holy Spirit's Indwelling Presence

> "And I will pray the Father, and He will give you another Helper, that He may abide with you forever,
> "even the Spirit of truth, whom the world cannot receive, because it neither sees Him nor knows Him; but

you know Him, for He dwells with you and will be in you...."

John 14:16-17 (NKJV)

Prays In Line With God's Perfect Will

Likewise the Spirit also helpeth our infirmities: for we know not what we should pray for as we ought: but the Spirit itself maketh intercession for us with groanings which cannot be uttered.

And he that searcheth the hearts knoweth what is the mind of the Spirit, because he maketh intercession for the saints according to the will of God.

Romans 8:26-27

Stimulates Faith

But ye, beloved, building up yourselves on your most holy faith, praying in the Holy Ghost.

Jude 1:20

Refreshes Spiritually

For with stammering lips and another tongue will he speak to this people.

To whom he said, This is the rest wherewith ye may cause the weary to rest; and this is the refreshing: yet they would not hear.

Isaiah 28:11-12

Opens Your Prayer Line To God

For he that speaketh in an unknown tongue speaketh not unto men, but unto God: for no man understandeth him; howbeit in the spirit he speaketh mysteries.

For if I pray in an unknown tongue, my spirit prayeth,

but my understanding is unfruitful.

1 Corinthians 14:2, 14

Please pray this prayer aloud now:

Father, thank You that at the moment I ask to be filled with the Holy Spirit, I will be filled. The evidence is that I will speak with other tongues by my will, though I will not understand with my mind. Now, Father, fill me with the Holy Spirit, in the Name of Jesus. Thank You for filling me. I have received, now. By a decision of my will, I speak to You in other tongues. In Jesus' Name. Amen.

We can build ourselves up and speak to God wherever we are—in the car, riding the bus or airplane, at home, or on the job. It will not disturb anyone. Speaking in tongues is a means of keeping free from the contamination of the world.

Supernatural Gifts Of Power

The gifts of the Holy Spirit can begin now to operate in and through your life. According to 1 Corinthians 12:7-11, the nine gifts of the Spirit are:

- Word of Wisdom
- Word of Knowledge
- Discerning of Spirits
- Prophecy
- Diversity of Tongues
- Interpretation of Tongues
- Special Faith
- Healings
- Working of Miracles

For more information about how to live as a victorious Christian, please order *The Victorious Walk* book. *Purchase this book wherever fine Christian products are sold in your area. Or, see the product list and order form at the back of this book.*

126

Pastor Gary invites you to:

Victory Christian Fellowship

One of the Fastest-Growing Churches on the U.S. East Coast!

SERVICE SCHEDULE

Sunday Morning	8:30 a.m.	Worship & Teaching
	11:00 a.m.	Worship & Teaching
Sunday Evening	6:00 p.m.	Water Baptism
	7:00 p.m.	Worship & Teaching
Wednesday	7:00 p.m.	Worship & Teaching

This church is dedicated to reaching out to meet your family's needs and to help you grow strong spiritually through the revelation knowledge of God's Word. Your faith will be strengthened as you see that Word in action! Visit today or call for prayer.

VICTORY CHRISTIAN FELLOWSHIP
100 Wilton Blvd.
New Castle, DE 19720   U.S.A.
PHONE: 1 (302) 324-5400
FAX: 1 (302) 324-5448
WEB SITE: www.gwwm.com

(On Rte. 40, just past the 13/40 split at Wilton.)

Pastor Gary V. Whetstone

What will you do with God's call on your life?

Find God's Answer Through:

School of Victorious Living

Face life's challenges with proven biblical answers!

Audio/video teachings with study guides available for study in your own home.

School of Biblical Studies

Establish a closer relationship with God!
Gain a deeper understanding of His Word.

An in-depth bible school curriculum for the serious student of God's Word.

School of Ministerial Training

Called into full-time ministry?
Pastor/Teacher · Evangelist/Missionary
Church Helps · Music Ministry

Receive hands-on training along with classroom instruction.

Products by Gary V. Whetstone

Purchase the following products where Christian products are sold in your area. Or order using the form at the end of this book.

Freedom Series

Assignment Against the Church: The Spirit of Offense
The demonic stronghold of the Prince of Offense and his diabolical plan to cripple the Body of Christ is exposed and dealt with in this life-changing tape series.

	6-tape audio	$ 35.00 VR001A

Blood-Bought Promises
Understand the awesome covenant that God has with you through the Blood of Jesus. These tapes provide a complete understanding of the terms, provision, and power of the covenant. Hold onto your seat...you never will relate to God or His provisions in the same way again!

Includes study guide	4-tape audio	$ 25.00 VR002A
Includes study guide	4-hour video	$ 65.00 VR002V

Breaking the Invisible Barriers
Do you feel that a wall of resistance has held you back? Learn how to break the barriers in your life and experience the power of breakthrough at a new level.

	4-tape audio	$ 25.00 VR012A

Discovering God's Highway to Your Destiny
God has an awesome plan for your life. The revelations that you will receive from this series will be life-changing as you travel on His expressway.

Includes study guide	4-tape audio	$ 25.00 VE006A

Extracting the Gold from Life's Crises
Learn how to correctly handle pressure, stress, conflict, and temptation so they work for your benefit! This series will teach you how to draw the wealth out of distresses in life by going THROUGH them in victory.

Includes study guide	4-tape audio	$ 25.00 VR003A
Includes study guide	4-hour video	$ 65.00 VR003V

Freedom from Insecurity and Inferiority— Crowned to Reign as a King
Do you struggle with insecurities and feelings of inferiority? Do the memories of your past seem to limit your future potential? This series will help you to experience freedom to reign as a king over your

perceived limitations.

Includes study guide	*6-tape audio*	*$ 35.00*	*VR004A*
Includes study guide	*6-hour video*	*$ 85.00*	*VR004V*

How to Stop Satan's Attack on God's Timing, Plans and Purposes

This course is an extraordinary, behind-the-scenes exposé of how Satan interferes with God's will for your life. Biblically, you will study the predestinated purpose, plan, and timing already set by God for you. Learn why these areas may not be working and how to stop the enemy "dead in his tracks."

9-tape audio	*$ 45.00*	*BM203A00*
Study guide	*$ 5.00*	*BM203S00*

Identify and Remove Curses

Unseen words spoken by you or others have restricted and limited your success in life. This series helps you to break the power of the curses that are working against you.

ISBN 0-9664462-1-6	*Paperback Book*	*$ 8.00*	*VR005B*
Includes study guide	*6-tape audio*	*$ 35.00*	*VR005A*
Includes study guide	*6-hour video*	*$ 85.00*	*VR005V*

The Journey from Frustration to Fulfillment

Are you living in frustration—knowing that God has a plan, purpose, and destiny in store for you but not yet fulfilling it? This series reveals how to remove the restrictions that have thwarted God's destiny for your life and gives an action plan that will lift you to a new level of purpose, excitement, and fulfillment in your life.

Includes study guide	*6-tape audio*	*$ 35.00* *VR006A*

Love's Transforming Power

God's love for us is awesome. This series will anchor you in the revelation of God's love that will transform you to become secure, moldable, and pliable in God's hands every moment of your life.

Includes study guide	*4-tape audio*	*$ 25.00*	*VR007A*
Includes study guide	*4-hour video*	*$ 65.00*	*VR007V*

Make Fear Bow

Experience an understanding of the causes of your fears that will enable you to break free from their bondage so you can live victoriously in God's promises.

ISBN 0-9664462-3-2	*Paperback Book*	*$ 8.00*	*VR008B*
Includes study guide	*4-tape audio*	*$ 25.00*	*VR008A*

The Power of the Lord's Blessing

Many believers are not experiencing God's blessing. This series reveals how to free yourself from Satan's barriers of frustration and self-effort. Break through to the blessings God has destined for you.

Includes study guide	*4-tape audio*	*$ 25.00* *VR009A*

Victory in Spiritual Warfare
This engaging and informative, yet shocking, revelation presents a comprehensive, biblical explanation of spiritual warfare, and teaches a practical and effective strategy for overcoming the work of evil spirits. Once the light of revelation comes, you will be able to identify, locate, and eradicate the power of the enemy.

ISBN 0-9664462-2-4	*Paperback Book*	$ 8.00	VR010B
	8-tape audio	$ 45.00	VR010A
	8-hour video	$ 99.00	VR010V

Victory in Spiritual Warfare Seminar
For those interested in further study of God's Word on identifying, locating, and destroying the works of darkness, this detailed, in-depth course, offered as a follow-up to the School of Victorious Living 8-tape *Victory in Spiritual Warfare* series, will fully equip you to live above every attack and plan of the enemy.

26-tape audio	$125.00	BM201A00
Comprehensive study guide	$ 13.00	BM103500

The Victorious Walk
This book covers the basic, foundational truths that are necessary for every believer to live victoriously.

ISBN 0-9664462-0-8	*Paperback Book*	$ 3.00	VR015B

VICTORY IN SPIRITUAL WARFARE

This exciting book is available wherever Christian products are sold in your area. Or, see the product list and order form at the back of this book. A dynamic testimony of deliverance as well as sound biblical teaching, this book will help believers who want to walk victoriously!

ISBN 0-9664462-2-4

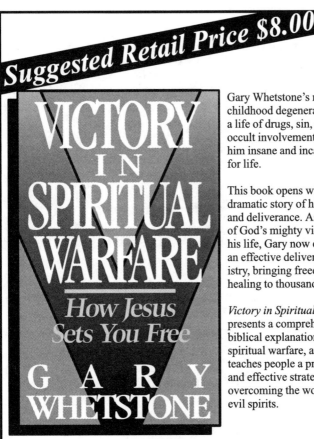

Gary Whetstone Worldwide Ministries
Product and Information Order Form

☐ Rev.   ☐ Mr.   ☐ Mrs.   ☐ Ms.   ☐ Miss   (Please print)

Name_____

Address_____

City_____ State_____ ZIP _____

Home Phone (____)_____ Work Phone (____)_____

Please send information about the following to me:
- ☐ Ministry Products (Catalog)
- ☐ Gary Whetstone Worldwide Ministries (Information and Itinerary)
- ☐ School of Victorious Living (Audio/video teachings)
- ☐ School of Biblical Studies (Delaware campuses or out-of-state sites)
- ☐ School of Biblical Studies (Audio-correspondence program)
- ☐ School of Ministerial Training (Delaware campus)
- ☐ Victory Christian Fellowship (Church)

☐ **Pastor Gary, please pray for me. I am enclosing my prayer needs on a separate page.**

☐ **Pastor Gary, enclosed on a separate sheet is my testimony of how this book and/or your ministry ministered to me.**

Please send the following products to me:

Quantity	Item #	Title	Price	Total
			$	$
			$	$
			$	$
			$	$

(U.S.A.) SHIPPING & HANDLING			
Up to $10.00....$1.50 $10.01-$50.00...$3.50 $50.01-Up.........$5.00	Subtotal	$	
	Shipping/Handling	$	
	TOTAL	$	

Credit Card: ☐MasterCard   ☐VISA   ☐American Express   ☐Discover

Account No._____

Expiration Date_____

Signature_____

Please make all checks payable in U.S. Dollars to "G.W.W.M."
Allow 4-6 weeks for delivery. No C.O.D.'s accepted.

Send your order and payment to:
Gary Whetstone Worldwide Ministries
P.O. Box 10050 • Wilmington, DE 19850 U.S.A.
PHONE: 1 (302) 324-5400 • FAX: 1 (302) 324-5448 • WEB SITE: www.gwwm.com

Gary Whetstone

Gary Whetstone is the Senior Pastor and Founder of Victory Christian Fellowship in New Castle, Delaware, and Founder of Gary Whetstone Worldwide Ministries.

Since personally experiencing God's miraculous deliverance and healing in 1971, Gary Whetstone has devoted his life to helping others become free. He ministers locally, nationally, and internationally in evangelistic crusades and to equip the Body of Christ for victory in spiritual warfare. Gifted in teaching, Gary Whetstone provides sound, biblical instruction and practical strategy for defeating the enemy in every area of life.

Through the local outreach of Victory Christian Fellowship, God has set free hundreds of thousands of people in salvations, Baptisms in the Holy Spirit, healings, and many other signs, wonders, and miracles. Having a great burden to minister to the local community, Pastor Gary Whetstone and his church have launched life-changing outreaches in several areas: HIV/AIDS; substance and alcohol abuse; inner-city community outreach centers; Saturday Sidewalk Sunday School; food and clothing outreach programs; and many large evangelistic campaigns, including dramatic productions such as "Jesus, Light of the World," which draws over 45,000 people annually.

Gary Whetstone's heart's desire is to see 1,000 missionaries placed on the mission field from his ministry. To accomplish that dream, he has established the School of Biblical Studies (a video Bible School) and the School of Ministerial Training. Currently, the video school has several hundred national and international locations, which were opened in cooperation with many local churches. Gary Whetstone also holds crusades internationally, which draw crowds of tens of thousands. For many, these crusades are their first opportunity to hear the Gospel of Jesus Christ. Pastor Gary also sends forth evangelism teams, which minister both locally and internationally.

Gary Whetstone has appeared on many national and international radio and television programs, and has authored key books, among which are *The Victorious Walk, Identify and Remove Curses, Make Fear Bow, Millionaire Mentality,* and his personal testimony of miraculous deliverance and healing in *Victory in Spiritual Warfare.* The large number of study guides he has produced are a testament to his gifting in practical biblical teaching and are available for use with his numerous video and audio teaching series.

God has gifted Pastor Gary Whetstone with an incredible business sense and ability, enabling him to publish a series of teachings from *Purchasing and Negotiations* to *Success in Business* and *Millionaire Mentality*, which has aired on his 14-year-long radio program, "Power Impact." This broadcast currently reaches an audience of over four million listeners on the East Coast of the United States.

Gary Whetstone and his wife, Faye, have a particularly dynamic testimony of a restored marriage, which achieved national attention and was the cover story in *Charisma* magazine. Gary and Faye now conduct annual Marriage Advance seminars for couples looking to deeply enrich their relationships.

Pastors Gary and Faye Whetstone recently celebrated their 26th wedding anniversary. Their two adult children, Eric and Laurie, along with daughter-in-law, Rebecca, and grandson, Isaiah, are involved actively in the local and international Whetstone ministry.

To arrange a speaking engagement for Gary or Faye Whetstone, please contact:

Gary Whetstone Worldwide Ministries
P.O. Box 10050
Wilmington, DE 19850 U.S.A.
PHONE: 1 (302) 324-5400
FAX: 1 (302) 324-5448
WEB SITE: www.gwwm.com